F. Kavanagh   C.L. Moore   C.E. Morris   A. Smith

TEAM UP
IN ENGLISH

STUDENT'S BOOK

Contents

Unit	Grammar	Vocabulary
1 What shall we do? p. 6	Personal object pronouns *love / like / hate* + *-ing* form Making arrangements Linkers (1)	Sports Adjectives
2 Let's plan our trip quickly p. 14	Present continuous Adverbs of manner	Adverbs of manner The weather
3 She was born in 1991! p. 22	*be* – Past simple (all forms) Dates Past time expressions	Ordinal numbers Months, seasons, and dates Jobs
1-3 Check Your Progress pp. 30-31	**Culture Spot 1:** Roman Britain pp. 110-111	
4 We stayed up late! p. 32	Past simple – Regular verbs (all forms)	Action verbs (1)
5 I didn't bring my camera! p. 40	Past simple – Irregular verbs (all forms)	Tourism Points of interest in a city
6 How far is it to Barcelona? p. 48	*How* + adjective Asking for and giving directions Prepositions of movement	Means of transport Adjectives to describe size and distance Directions Places in the city
4-6 Check Your Progress pp. 56-57	**Culture Spot 2:** Cities, Towns and Villages pp. 112-113	

Communication / Pronunciation	Skills / CLIL / Curiosity Corner	Personal Toolkit
Talking about likes and dislikes Suggesting, accepting, refusing Word stress	**Skills** **Listening:** understanding actions in progress **Speaking:** talking about favourites **Reading:** identifying information in an SMS **Writing:** writing an e-mail to invite someone to do something	**Grammar** Pers. object pronouns p. 53 *-ing* form (gerund) p. 57 Making arrangements p. 142 Linkers (1) p. 52
Describing actions Talking about the weather Rhyming words (1)	**CLIL** Computer Safety	**Grammar** Present continuous p. 60 Adverbs of manner p. 23 **Pictionary** 7 Summer and Winter Clothes
Talking about dates and places of birth Talking about events in the past (1) The sound /θ/ for *-th*	**Curiosity Corner** Joke Time, Odd Jobs, Did you know?, General Knowledge Quiz, Weather Sayings, Cool Thought	**Grammar** *be* – Past simple p. 63 **Pictionary** 8 Jobs and Professions
Talking about a past holiday Talking about events in the past (2) Pronunciation of *-ed*: /d/, /t/, /ɪd/	**Skills** **Listening:** listening to a radio programme and identifying the essential information in a biography **Speaking:** interacting in a simulated interview **Reading:** identify the essential information in an interview **Writing:** writing a short story	**Grammar** Past simple – Regular verbs pp. 65-70
Talking about events in the past (3) Talking about a trip Intonation of questions	**CLIL** Discovering Food	**Grammar** Past simple – Irregular verbs pp. 67-70
Talking about length of journey with different means of transport Talking about size and distance Asking for and giving directions Sentence stress (1)	**Curiosity Corner** Did you know?, Joke Time, Incredible!, Post Facts, UK Tourist Attractions, Summer Holidays, Wordsearch, Question Time	**Grammar** *How* + adjective p. 32 Prepositions of movement p. 43 The imperative pp. 44-45 Means of transport p. 55 **Pictionary** 2 Positions 9 The Town in Winter and in Summer

Contents

Unit	Grammar	Vocabulary
7 Barcelona is better... p. 58	Comparatives	Adjectives to describe physical appearance and personality Adjectives to describe places and things
8 The best holiday ever p. 66	Superlatives Possessive pronouns	Natural and urban landscapes Adjectives to describe landscapes and personal objects
9 She was sitting next to you p. 74	Past continuous (all forms) Past simple vs Past continuous Linkers (2)	Prepositions of place Furniture and objects in a house Places in a public park
7-9 Check Your Progress pp. 82-83	**Culture Spot 3:** British History Timeline pp. 114-115	
10 We could join a club p. 84	can - ability can / could - permission and requests could - possibility could - short answers	Road signs Action verbs (2)
11 Everybody likes parties p. 92	*someone, anything, everywhere*, etc. Verb *get* Verbs + *-ing* form	Parties Expressions with *get*
12 Are you coming back? p. 100	*going to* future Present continuous for the future *going to* vs Present continuous	Action verbs (3) Computer words
10-12 Check Your Progress pp. 108-109	**Culture Spot 4:** Sports in the English-Speaking World pp. 116-117	

Communication / Pronunciation	Skills / CLIL / Curiosity Corner	Personal Toolkit
Talking about physical appearance and personality Making comparisons (1) Differences in pronunciation of *as*: /æz/ vs /əz/	**Skills** **Listening:** identifying the essential information in a conversation; understanding the description of a city, of a boy or a girl **Speaking:** interacting to compare personal preferences **Reading:** identifying the essential information in a descriptive text **Writing:** writing a personal descriptive text	**Grammar** Comparatives pp. 24-25 **Pictionary** 6 The Human Body
Making comparisons (2) Talking about objects you possess The sound /h/	**CLIL** Electricity and Lightning	**Grammar** Superlatives p. 26 Possessive pronouns p. 37 **Pictionary** 11 Our environment
Talking about position Talking about actions in progress in the past Talking on the telephone Rhyming words (2)	**Curiosity Corner** Did you know?, Joke Time, Incredible!, Riddle Time, Fun Fact, Wordsearch, Animal Crazy!, As slow as a snail!, Animal Quiz	**Grammar** Past continuous pp. 71-74 Linkers (2) p. 75 **Pictionary** 4 Moving House
Talking about permission to do something Making requests Rhyming words (3)	**Skills** **Listening:** identifying information to complete a brochure **Speaking:** interacting in a dialogue to ask about and express preferences **Reading:** grasping information from an advertisement **Writing:** writing a tourist brochure	**Grammar** Modal verbs: *can / could* pp. 100-101, 109 *lend / borrow* p. 137
Organising a party Talking about parties Sentence stress (2)	**CLIL** Earthquakes	**Grammar** *someone*, etc. *get* + adj. / past part. p. 122 Verbs and adj. + *-ing* form p. 58
Expressing intention Talking about plans /n/ vs /ŋ/	**Curiosity Corner** Joke Time, Wordsearch, Did you know?, UK Holiday Quiz, Experiment Time, Guess the Meaning, Shopaholics, Joke Time	**Grammar** The future pp. 82, 84-86

1 What shall we do?

1 Listen and read.

I love horse riding!

Sara: Look guys... what shall we do? There's cycling, swimming, sailing...
Francesco: What about snowboarding? I quite like snowboarding.
Asim: Yes, but snowboarding is a winter sport!
Francesco: Well, let's do something different... rock climbing or canoeing?
Asim: What do you think Sara?
Sara: Oh, I hate canoeing and I don't like the idea of rock climbing. It's really scary!
Francesco: It's not scary. It's great. I love it!
Sara: No, let's have a game of tennis. I like playing tennis.
Francesco: Oh, no! I hate tennis! There's too much running about and getting hot!
Asim: I don't mind tennis but we always play it at home. I play every Saturday with my sister. How about going horse riding?
Sara: Yeah, brilliant! I love horse riding.

Comprehension

2 Look at the emoticons showing Francesco's likes and dislikes, and complete the table for Asim and Sara. Use a question mark when you don't know the answer.

	rock climbing	canoeing	horse riding	playing tennis	snowboarding
Francesco	:))	?	?	:((	:)
Asim					
Sara					

Vocabulary

3 Match the activities to the pictures. Then listen and check.

- A athletics
- B tennis
- C basketball
- D gymnastics
- E swimming
- F horse riding
- G martial arts
- H rollerblading
- I sailing
- J ~~cricket~~
- K water polo
- L windsurfing

 J    1 ☐    2 ☐    3 ☐

 4 ☐    5 ☐    6 ☐    7 ☐

 8 ☐    9 ☐    10 ☐    11 ☐

Hot Tip!

For sports we use:
play: *play football, volleyball, tennis...*
go: *go cycling, sailing...*
do: *do martial arts, gymnastics...*

4 Write *play*, *do* or *go*. Then listen and check.

_do_ athletics
1 _____ tennis
2 _____ basketball
3 _____ gymnastics
4 _____ swimming
5 _____ horse riding
6 _____ martial arts
7 _____ rollerblading
8 _____ sailing
9 _____ cricket
10 _____ water polo
11 _____ windsurfing

Communication

Look & Use

I **like** play**ing** tennis.
I **don't mind** tennis.
I **hate** canoe**ing**.

5 Match the words and phrases to the icons. Then work in pairs and talk about your favourite sports and free-time activities.

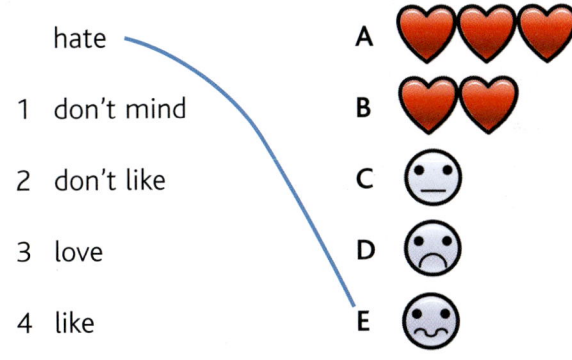

A *I love doing gymnastics.*
B *I hate swimming.*

My Turn

6 Work in pairs. Ask questions about your favourite activities. Take notes.

A *Do you like playing football?*
B *Yes, I do.*

A *Do you like doing gymnastics?*
B *No, I don't.*

7 Now write a short paragraph using your partner's answers in exercise 6. Link the sentences with *and*, *but* and *or*.

*Lisa doesn't like playing football **or** basketball **but** she loves playing tennis **and** volleyball.*

seven **7**

1

 **1** Listen and read.

Why don't we play them?

Sara:	What a horrible day! What can we do with our guests today?
Mrs Doyle:	Well, we've got some new board games. Why don't we play them?
Jack:	BORING!
Sara:	How about a treasure hunt? They're great fun!
Mrs Doyle:	I'm not sure.
Jack:	No, I don't like treasure hunts because they're too much work!
Mrs Doyle:	OK, what then? Our guests want to know what's happening on their last day at the Camp. What shall we do?
Jack:	Why don't we watch a film in the TV room?
Mrs Doyle:	That's a great idea, Jack!
Sara:	TV? No, thank you!
Jack:	What about a quiz? Or why don't we take photos for the Camp photo album?
Sara:	Brilliant idea!
Mrs Doyle:	Well done, Jack. And now I think it's time for a nice cup of tea.

Comprehension

2 Read the dialogue again and tick (✓) the correct statement.

1   ☐ **A** Sara doesn't know it's a horrible day.
    ☐ **B** Mrs Doyle and Sara know it's a horrible day.
2   ☐ **A** Jack thinks board games are boring.
    ☐ **B** Mrs Doyle thinks board games are boring.
3   ☐ **A** Sara wants a treasure hunt because it's fun.
    ☐ **B** Jack doesn't want a treasure hunt because it's too noisy.
4   ☐ **A** Sara likes the idea of watching a film.
    ☐ **B** Mrs Doyle likes the idea of watching a film.

3 Look at the dialogue and complete the table with expressions for suggesting, accepting or refusing an idea.

Suggesting	Accepting	Refusing
Why don't we play them?		

8   eight

Vocabulary

4 Match the adjectives to the pictures.

> dangerous   scary
> exciting   ~~boring~~
> fun   tiring

boring

1 _____

2 _____   3 _____

4 _____   5 _____

Communication

Look & Use

What **can** we do?
What **shall** we do?
Why don't we play them?
Shall we play board games?
What about a quiz?

5 Work in pairs. Look at the picture and ask questions.

A *Shall we go running?*
B *No, that's boring!*
A *Why don't we play tennis?*
B *Yes! I think tennis is fun!*

Sounds Good!

 6 Listen and underline the stressed syllable.

cycling   canoeing
swimming   tennis
snowboarding   horse riding
rock climbing   football

 **7** Listen again and repeat.

My Turn

8 Interview two classmates and take notes. Write sentences about their likes and dislikes using *because*.

A *How about playing board games?*
B *No, that's boring!*

> Annie doesn't like board games
> **because** they are boring.

1 Grammar Focus

Personal object pronouns

Read the examples and complete the table.

Do you like rock climbing?
*I love **it**!*

Do you like board games?
*No, I hate **them**!*

*We always listen to **you**, but you never listen to **us**!*

Subject pronouns	Object pronouns
I	me
you	_____
he	him
she	her
it	it
we	_____
you	you
they	_____

Now read these examples, then choose the correct option.

*Please give the CD **to him**!*
*This is my new **car**. I like **it**.*
*I don't eat **tomatoes**. I don't like **them**.*
*Call Sara, please. There's an e-mail **for her**.*
*Be quiet and listen **to me**.*

We use personal object pronouns **after** a **verb** (direct object) or after a *noun / preposition* (indirect object).

1 Complete the sentences with the correct object pronouns.

   A Do you like coffee?
   B No, I don't like __it__. (coffee)
1 A Do you see your grandparents very often?
   B No, not often but they come to visit _____ every Christmas. (our family)
2 A Where are my shoes?
   B The dog has got _____! (my shoes)
3 A There's a letter for Nick.
   B I can give it to _____. (Nick)
4 A Mrs Maigret is our new French teacher.
   B Do you like _____? (the teacher)

2 Complete the dialogues with the correct subject or object pronouns.

1 A I think your brother is nice. I like _____!
   B I don't! _____'s boring!
2 A Do you like vegetables?
   B No, I don't. _____'re horrible.
   A Silly boy! I like _____ a lot.
3 A I love rock climbing. _____'s exciting!
   B I don't like _____. I think _____'s scary.
4 A This is Julia, my best friend. I like _____. I think _____'s a lovely person.

love / like / hate + -ing form

Read the examples, then choose the correct option.

*I love swimm**ing**.*
*I like snowboard**ing**.*
*I don't like rock climb**ing**.*
*I hate going shopp**ing**.*

After verbs expressing likes and dislikes we use a noun or the *base form / -ing form* (gerund) of the verb.

> **PT Grammar**
> ----▶ Pers. object pron. p. 53 ----▶ Making arrangements p. 142
> ----▶ -ing form (gerund) p. 57 ----▶ Linkers (1) p. 52

3 Complete the sentences with the correct form of the verbs in the box.

> ~~play~~ go ~~watch~~ drink
> live read get up

- A Does Steven like _playing_ football?
- B No, he doesn't, but he loves _watching_ it.
1. A Does Lucy like _____ in the morning?
   B No, she doesn't, but she likes _____ to bed late.
2. A What kind of books do you like _____?
   B I like thrillers and science fiction.
3. A Do cats like _____ milk?
   B Yes, they love it.
4. A Do they like _____ in their town?
   B Yes, they do, because they can go swimming every day in the sea.

Making arrangements

Asking for suggestions

> **Write these questions in your language.**
>
> What shall we do?
> _____
>
> What do you want to do?
> _____
>
> What can we do?
> _____
>
> We use these questions when we want to ask for **suggestions** about what to do.

Making suggestions

> **Read the two dialogues on pages 6 and 8 and find examples for these forms of making suggestions.**
>
> 1 *Why don't we* + base form of the verb + *?*
>   _____
>
> 2 *What about* + *-ing* form (gerund) of the verb + *?*
>   _____
>
> 3 *How about* + *-ing* form of the verb + *?*
>   _____
>
> 4 *Let's* + base form of the verb.
>   _____

4 Work in pairs. Use the prompts and make suggestions. You can accept (✓) or refuse (✗). When you refuse, make a different suggestion.

> play tennis (✗)
> A *Why don't we play tennis?*
> B *No, I hate tennis! What about running in the park?*

1. go to the shopping centre (✓)
2. watch a horror film on TV (✗)
3. have a sandwich (✓)
4. organise a party (✓)
5. do martial arts (✗)

Linkers (1)

> **Read the examples and complete the rules.**
>
> *I like swimming **and** horse riding.*
> *I like athletics **but** I hate gymnastics.*
> *He doesn't like tennis **or** basketball.*
> *They like sailing **because** it's great fun.*
>
> We use:
>
> _____ to link similar ideas
> _____ to link contrasting ideas
> ___or___ to link alternative ideas
> _____ to talk about reason

eleven **11**

1 Skills

Listening

1 Listen to the dialogues and tick (✓) the correct answer.

1 What is Julia doing now?

A ☐   B ☐   C ☐

2 What is the boy listening to?

A ☐   B ☐   C ☐

3 What are the people doing?

A ☐   B ☐   C ☐

4 What is the dog doing?

A ☐   B ☐   C ☐

2 Listen to the interview and tick (✓) T (True) or F (False).

		T	F
1	Fiona loves watching TV.	☐	☐
2	*The O.C.* is her favourite programme.	☐	☐
3	She doesn't like Ryan.	☐	☐
4	She loves animals.	☐	☐
5	She's got four dogs and four cats.	☐	☐
6	She usually goes to the seaside with her pets.	☐	☐

Speaking

3 What's your favourite sport? Who's your favourite singer? Write your favourites. Then ask your partner and complete the table with his / her favourites.

- A *I love playing volleyball. And you? What's your favourite sport?*
- B *I like doing gymnastics.*
- A *My favourite actress is Keira Knightley. Do you like her?*
- B *No, I don't. I like Jessica Alba.*

	My favourite	Your favourite
Sport		
Film		
Book		
Singer / Group		
Actor / Actress		

4 In small groups, discuss your favourites.

- A *Does Lisa like Jessica Alba?*
- B *No, she doesn't. She likes Keira Knightley.*

Keira Knightley   Jessica Alba

Reading

5 Read the text message about Miriam's party and answer the questions.

1. Who is writing the text? _____
2. Who is receiving the text? _____
3. Where is Jane? _____
4. What can Mike bring? _____
5. What is great? _____

Hi Mike! ☺
Where R U? Brilliant party at Miriam's! Y don't U come? Bring food or drink! The music is great! See U soon.
Jane

Writing

6 Write an e-mail to your friend and invite him / her to do something interesting for the weekend.

2 Let's plan our trip quickly

1 Listen and read.

We miss our friends!

Mrs Doyle:	Hey kids, why are you sitting here indoors? What's up? You're usually outside at this time.
David:	We miss our friends!
Mrs Doyle:	I can't stand seeing you so sad. I've got an idea! Why don't we go and visit your friends?
Jack:	Really? But how?
Mrs Doyle:	We can drive. There are four of us, and Emi. A camper van is a good idea.
David:	Where do we get a camper van?
Mrs Doyle:	We can hire one. They're not expensive.
Sara:	Great! David has got a driving licence and you can drive really well too.
Mrs Doyle:	Of course!
Sara:	Hurrah! Let's plan our trip quickly.
Mrs Doyle:	What about going to France first?
Sara:	Yes, then let's go to Italy and then Spain and...
Mrs Doyle:	OK, OK! Let's do this slowly!
David:	Oh, it's so exciting!
Emi:	Woof!

Comprehension

2 Read the following sentences and tick (✓) T (True), F (False) or DS (Doesn't Say).

		T	F	DS
	David is waiting for a phone call.	☐	☐	✓
1	They miss their friends.	☐	☐	☐
2	David has got an idea.	☐	☐	☐
3	Camper vans are expensive to hire.	☐	☐	☐
4	David can drive well.	☐	☐	☐
5	Their first destination is Spain.	☐	☐	☐
6	David thinks the idea is boring.	☐	☐	☐

2

Vocabulary

3 Look at the pictures and write the correct adverbs.

~~clumsily~~   quickly   hard   comically
loudly   well   carelessly

move *clumsily*

1 talk _____

2 cook _____

3 act _____

4 run _____

¡Hola! ¿Qué tal?
5 speak Spanish
_____

6 study _____

4 Listen and check.

Communication

Look & Use

You can drive really **well**.
Let's plan our trip **quickly**.
Let's do this **slowly**!

5 Ask and answer questions about the pictures using the prompts.

move
quickly / slowly

A *Is the car moving slowly?*
B *No, it isn't. It's moving quickly.*

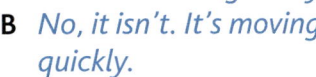
1 sing
well / badly
_____
_____

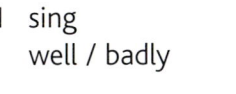

2 speak
loudly / quietly
_____
_____

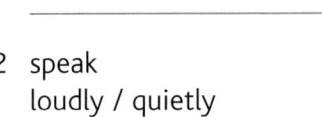

3 drive
carelessly / carefully
_____
_____

4 walk
sadly / happily
_____
_____

My Turn

6 Write five sentences about how you can do things and tell your partner. Then discuss them together.

A *I can run quickly.*
B *No, you can't. You run very slowly! / Yes, I know.*

fifteen **15**

2

1 Listen and read.

Oh no! It's raining!

Sara: Oh no! It's raining... and it's cold! We can't play games outside today!
Jack: Listen! There's thunder and look, lightning too!
Mrs Doyle: Don't say that Jack! My washing is drying on the line.
David: I think it's getting wet in this stormy weather.
Mrs Doyle: Oh well. Let's have a cup of tea then!
Sara: That's your answer to everything!
Jack: I wonder what the weather is like in Spain today.
David: Oh, cool. José's in Spain! We can look it up on the Internet.

David gets his laptop out.

Jack: Oh lucky thing! It's really hot and sunny in Madrid.
Sara: What's the weather like in Rome?
David: It's hot but cloudy and windy in Rome and guess what? It's snowing in Japan. Poor Sumi!
Mrs Doyle: What about New York?

Comprehension

2 Tick (✓) the correct answer.

Mrs Doyle's washing is
- [ ] A drying on the line.
- [✓] B getting wet on the line.
- [ ] C not on the line.

1 Mrs Doyle's answer to everything is
- [ ] A to have a sandwich.
- [ ] B to have a cup of tea.
- [ ] C to have a cup of coffee.

2 José
- [ ] A lives in Rome.
- [ ] B doesn't live in Paris.
- [ ] C lives in Spain.

3 In Japan
- [ ] A it's raining.
- [ ] B it's hot.
- [ ] C it's snowing.

4 Mrs Doyle
- [ ] A thinks that it's windy and cloudy in New York.
- [ ] B asks about the weather in New York.
- [ ] C thinks it's snowing in New York.

Vocabulary

3 Match the symbols to the words. Then listen and check.

cloudy   cold   ~~foggy~~   hot   raining
snowing   stormy   sunny   warm   windy

 It's *foggy*

 5 It's _____.

 1 It's _____.

 6 It's _____.

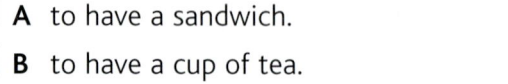 2 It's _____.

 7 It's _____.

 3 It's _____.

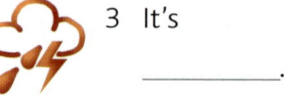 8 It's _____.

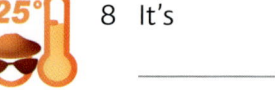 4 It's _____.

 9 It's _____.

Communication

Look & Use

What's the weather **like** in Rome?
It's hot but cloudy and windy.

A *What's the weather like in Edinburgh today?*
B *It's cloudy but it's warm.*

4 Listen and complete the weather forecast. Then work in pairs and use the information to ask and answer questions.

	☀	🌧	❄	🥶	⛈	☁	25°
Edinburgh						✓	✓
Birmingham							
Glasgow							
Plymouth							
Swansea							
Southampton							

5 Work in pairs. Student B: look at the map on page 118.
Student A: look at the map below and read the weather forecast to Student B. Then listen to Student B and draw the correct weather symbols on the cities.

Today it's sunny in Manchester...

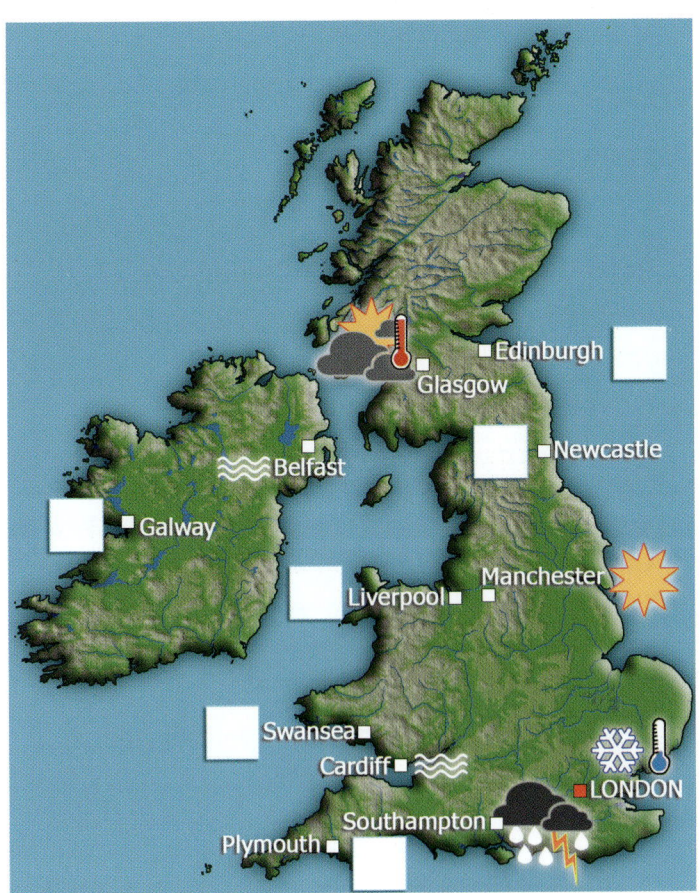

Sounds Good!

6 Listen to these silly sentences about the weather and fill in the gaps. Then check in pairs.

The _snow_ is cold when you're old.
1 I'm n_____ h_____!
2 There's a w_____ st_____ in the m_____.
3 The r_____ in S_____ is a real p_____.
4 M_____ e_____ is very d_____!

My Turn

7 Look at this map of Italy. Draw the symbols and then tell your partner what the weather is like on your map.

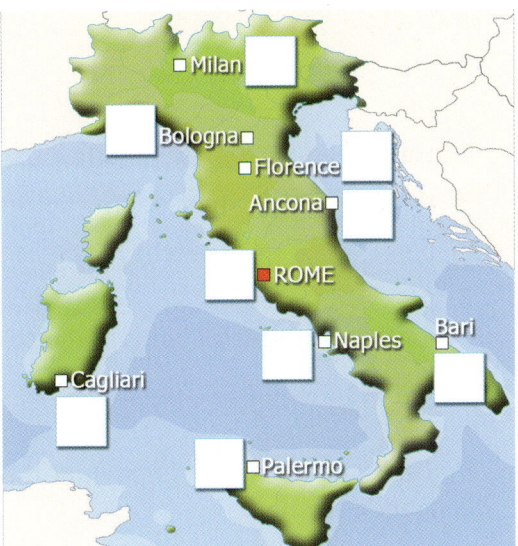

seventeen 17

2 Grammar Focus

Present continuous

We use the present continuous to talk about what is happening now.

Read the two dialogues on pages 14 and 16. Underline examples of the present continuous, then complete the rule.

In the present continuous the sentence pattern is:

subject + present simple of verb _____ + _____ form of the main verb.

Sara _____ play _____.

What happens when we add -ing to a verb? Look at the examples and complete the spelling rules.

Sara is sit**ting**.
Mrs Doyle is mak**ing** tea.
We love canoe**ing**.

For **one-syllable** verbs ending in single vowel + single consonant we double the last consonant and add _____.

For verbs ending in **silent -e** we drop the -e and add _____.

We don't drop the final **-e** when it isn't silent.

1 Complete the sentences with the present continuous of the verbs in brackets.

She _is listening_ (listen) to her new CD.

1 He _____ (sit) on the bus.
2 I _____ (not do) my homework, I _____ (watch) TV!
3 Alex and James _____ (play) football with their friends in the park.
4 Helen's mum _____ (make) dinner.
5 They _____ (study) for the French exam.

2 Look at the picture. Tick (✓) T (True) or F (False). Correct the false sentences.

	T	F
Will and Tom are drinking coffee.	☐	✓

Will and Tom aren't drinking coffee. They're eating cake.

1 Frank is sleeping. ☐ ☐
2 Melissa is dancing. ☐ ☐
3 Emma is reading a magazine. ☐ ☐
4 Paul is watching TV. ☐ ☐
5 Holly and Louise are eating cake. ☐ ☐

Adverbs of manner

Read the examples and underline the adverbs.

They are speaking quietly.
He's driving carefully.
Don't drive dangerously!
I'm sitting comfortably.

Circle the correct option and get the rules.

We use adverbs of manner to express *how / why* we do something.

To form adverbs of manner we generally add **-ly** to *adjectives / nouns*.

2

PT Grammar
---▶ Pres. continuous p. 60
---▶ Adverbs of manner p. 23

Adverbs of manner
Spelling

Look at the examples and complete the rules.

quick	→	quick**ly**
slow	→	slow**ly**
serious	→	serious**ly**
careful	→	careful**ly**

We generally add ____ to regular adjectives.

| happy | → | happ**ily** |
| pretty | → | prett**ily** |

For adjectives ending in **-y** we drop the ____ and add **-ily**.

| sensible | → | sensi**bly** |
| comfortable | → | comforta**bly** |

For adjectives ending in **-ble** we drop the **e** and add ____.

| comic | → | comic**ally** |
| tragic | → | tragic**ally** |

For adjectives ending in **-ic** we add ____.

| good | → | well |
| fast | → | fast |

Some adjectives are irregular.

Position of adverbs

Read the examples, then circle the correct option.

*They are waiting **patiently**.*
*Is she reading **carefully**?*
*We aren't walking **quickly**.*

Adverbs of manner generally go *after / before* the verb.

3 Complete the sentences with the adverb of the adjectives in the box. Then match them to the correct pictures.

comfortable   dangerous   happy   ~~quiet~~   strange

A The children are sitting very _____. [B]

B Please speak _quietly_. The baby is sleeping! [1]

C They are living _____ together in their new house. [2]

D Sam is acting _____ at the moment. [3]

E That man is driving _____! [4]

4 Sara is describing a photo. Complete the description. Use the -ing form of the verbs and change the adjectives into adverbs.

Look at the picture! There I am _smiling happily_ (smile / happy) because our new guests are here.
Natalie and Francesco are (1) _____ _____ (talk / loud) and Paolo is (2) _____ _____ (wait / patient) for a chance to speak. Emi is (3) _____ her tail _____ (wag / happy).

CLIL Computer Safety

Internet Safety

1 What do you use the Internet for?

2 Do you know what 'www' means? Look at the pictures and complete the words to find out.

W _ R _ D

W I _ E

W _ B

Remember the Internet can be dangerous too!

3 Read the contract and tick (✓) *Do* or *Don't*. Then compare with your partner.

FAMILY CONTRACT for ONLINE SAFETY

	Do	Don't
Give out personal information (address, telephone number, parents' work address/telephone number, or the name and location of my school) without my parents' permission.	☐	✓
Tell my parents if I find information or messages that disturb me.	✓	☐
Agree to meet in person someone I 'meet' online.	☐	☐
Send my picture without asking my parents.	☐	☐
Decide with my parents when I can be online.	☐	☐
Decide with my parents for how long I can be online.	☐	☐
Ask my parents before downloading or installing software.	☐	☐
Be a good 'online citizen' and don't do anything that hurts other people or is against the law.	☐	☐

I PROMISE I WILL NEVER BREAK THESE RULES.

Student sign here   Parent sign here
_____   _____

4 Listen and check.

Project Time

Create a poster about Online Safety using information from this page and your own ideas.

Computer Games

1 Work in pairs. How many computer game titles do you know in English?

2 Ask and answer the questions in pairs.

1	Do you like computer games?	☐ Yes, I do. ☐ No, I don't.
2	What kind of computer games do you play? ☐ strategy ☐ action ☐ role playing ☐ cards ☐ sport	
3	What's your favourite game?	My favourite game is _____
4	How often do you play computer games? I play ☐ every day ☐ once a week ☐ twice a week ☐ _____	
5	How long do you play each time?	☐ ___ minutes ☐ ___ hours
6	How many hours do you think is enough per day?	_____

Too much time playing computer games may cause problems.

C 1.15 3 Match the problems with the remedies. Then listen and check.

PROBLEM

1 D Headache.
   ☐

2 ☐ Carpal tunnel syndrome (an aching wrist).

3 ☐ Tired eyes.
   ☐

4 ☐ Backache.
   ☐

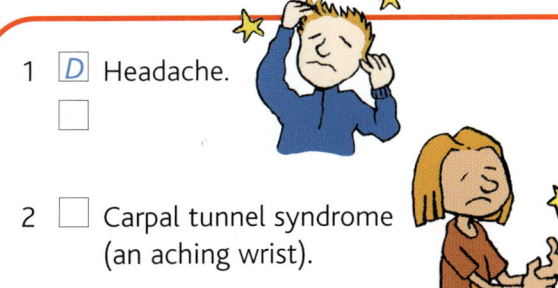

REMEDY

A Stay 45 to 60 centimetres away from the screen.

B Use a wrist rest.

C Keep your back straight.

D̶ Do not spend more than 30 minutes without a break.

E Give your eyes a rest: look out of a window.

F Give your body a break: move your muscles.

G Limit yourself to 1-2 hours of screen time per day.

Project Time

Create a wall chart with graphs for your classroom about computer games. Use the results from the questionnaire in exercise 2.

3 She was born in 1991!

1 Listen and read.

When were you born?

Jack: David! Look at Sara's passport!
David: What's the matter with it?
Jack: She was born on 23rd December 1991. She's old!
David: Don't be silly! She's not old.
Jack: You're only saying that because *you're* really old David! When were you born?
Sara: I know! Your birthday is in the summer, in August. There was a big party last year.
David: Yeah, that's right. I was born on 14th August 1986.
Jack: See! He's old!
Sara: So when were you born then baby?
Jack: My birthday's in the spring. It's in April.
David: Jack's an April fool! He was born on April 1st 1997.
Jack: Oh very funny!
Sara: And I was an early Christmas present!
David: So... I was born in the summer, Jack in the spring and Sara in the winter. Wasn't Emi born in the autumn, Jack?
Jack: Yes, she was born on 30th September 2006. She's the real baby!

Comprehension

2 Complete the sentences.

Sara's birthday is on _23rd December_.

1 There was a big birthday party for _____ last year.
2 Jack was born on _____.
3 _____ was an early Christmas present!
4 Emi was born in the _____ on 30th September 2006.

22 twenty-two

Vocabulary

3 Match the months of the year to the correct season.

November January July December
September February June March
October April August May

SPRING	SUMMER
_____	_____
_____	_____
_____	_____

AUTUMN	WINTER
_____	_____
_____	_____
_____	_____

4 Read the dialogue on page 22 again and match the names to the birthdays.

23rd December — Jack
14th August — Sara
30th September — Emi
1st April — David

Sounds Good!

5 The sound /θ/ for -th. Listen and repeat.
fifth   eleventh   fifteenth   tenth

6 Now listen and write the ordinal numbers you hear in the four dialogues.

1 _____   2 _____
3 _____   4 _____

Communication

Look & Use

When **were** you **born**?
I **was born** on 14th August 1986.
When **was** Sara **born**?
She **was born** on 23rd December 1991.

7 Guess the famous people's birthdays. Then ask and answer questions in pairs.

26th August 1910   21st June 1982
2nd October 1869   22nd November 1984

Mahatma Gandhi   Scarlett Johansson

Mother Teresa   Prince William

A *When was... born?*
B *He / She was born on...*

My Turn

8 Ask and answer the questions in pairs.

1 A Which month is it now? B It's...
2 A Which month was it last month?
  B It was...
3 A Which season is it now? B It's...
4 A When is your teacher's birthday?
  B It's in...
5 A When were you born?
  B I was born on...
6 A Which is your favourite season and why?
  B It's... because...

3

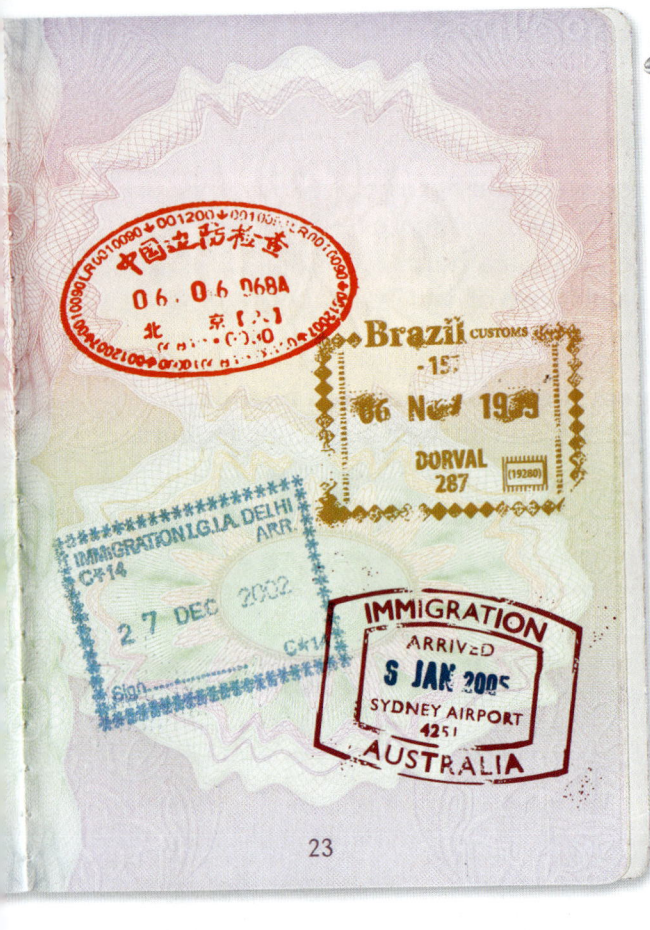

 1 Listen and read.

When was that?

Jack: Wow, Mrs Doyle. Your passport is amazing. Look at all these stamps!
Mrs Doyle: Yes, there was Brazil...
Sara: Brazil? Really? When was that?
Mrs Doyle: It was a long time ago in November 1989.
Sara: Oh, I'd love to go! Were there lots of white sandy beaches?
Mrs Doyle: Yes, there were!
David: And what about this one? Were you in China in 2002?
Mrs Doyle: No, I wasn't. I was a tour guide in India in December 2002.
Jack: But weren't you in Australia in 2002?
Mrs Doyle: No, that was in 2005. It was wonderful!
David: So when were you in China?
Mrs Doyle: We were there in June 1999.
All: WE?
Sara: You mean there was someone with you?
Mrs Doyle: Well yes, actually, there was.
Jack: But who were you with?!

Comprehension

2 Read the dialogue again and match the places to the months and years.

Australia	June	2002
Brazil	January	1999
China	December	1989
India	November	2005

Vocabulary

 3 Match the jobs to the pictures, then listen and check.

<del>architect</del>
tour guide
lawyer
pilot
singer
doctor
office worker
factory worker

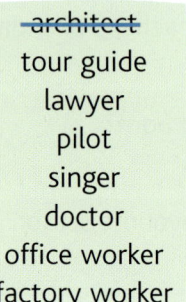 architect  1 _____  2 _____  3 _____

 4 _____  5 _____  6 _____  7 _____

Communication

Look & Use

Were there lots of sandy beaches?
Yes, there were.

Were you in China in 2002?
No, I wasn't.

When were you in China?
We were there in 1999.

4 Look at Mrs Doyle's scrap book from her trip to Australia. In pairs, ask and answer questions.

   a lot of people on the trip?
A *Were there a lot of people on the trip?*
B *Yes, there were.*

1 tour guide / boring?
2 architect / French?
3 koalas / funny?
4 Queen Elizabeth / opening of the Opera House?
5 weather / cold?

My Turn

5 Student A: go to page 119. Student B: go to page 120.

3 Grammar Focus

be – Past simple

Affirmative, negative and questions

Complete the table with the missing forms.

Affirmative form	Negative form	Questions
I was	I wasn't	Was I...?
You were	You weren't	_____
He was	_____	Was he...?
She was	_____	_____
It was	It wasn't	Was it...?
We were	We weren't	_____
You were	_____	_____
They were	_____	Were they...?

Look at the table then complete the rules.

The past simple of the verb *be* has two forms.

We use _____ after *I / he / she / it*.
We use _____ after *you / we / they*.

In the negative form we add _____ .
In questions the verb goes _____ the subject.

Short answers

Read the examples and complete the pattern.

Were you in China in 1999?
Yes, I **was**.

Was the tour guide boring?
No, she **wasn't**.

In short answers the sentence pattern is:
Yes, + subject + _____ / were.
No, + subject + _____ / weren't.

1 Complete the sentences with *was / were* or *wasn't / weren't*.

The party _was_ great!
1 Susi and Dan _____ at school yesterday. They were at home.
2 It's hot today but it _____ cold yesterday.
3 Kafka _____ born in England.
4 The Beatles _____ an English group.

2 Complete the questions and write short answers.

A _Were_ you at school at 9 o'clock this morning? (✓)
B *Yes, we were.*

1 A _____ blue her favourite colour when she was a child? (✗)
  B _____ .
2 A _____ Tom and Jerry their favourite cartoon characters when they were children? (✓)
  B _____ .
3 A _____ Shakespeare a dancer? (✗)
  B _____ .
4 A _____ you and your friends at the library yesterday? (✓)
  B _____ .

Read the examples and complete the rules.

Were you in China? No, I wasn't. I was in India.

Oscar Wilde **was** an Irish writer.

Were there lots of white sandy beaches?
Yes, there were.

We use the _____ to talk about a completed action or situation in the past.

There is and *there are* become *there was* and *there* _____ in the past.

Dates

Think and answer.
In English we generally use ordinal numbers to say dates. Is it the same in your language? ____

Read the examples and write how we say the last two dates.

We write	We say
3rd June	**the** third **of** June
on 14th August	on **the** fourteenth **of** August
on April 1st	on April **the** first / on **the** first **of** April
30th May	on **the** thirtieth **of** May
11th November	_____
18th March	_____

Read the rule and complete.
For the years up to 1999 we say:
1492 = 14 92 = *fourteen ninety-two*
1865 = 18 65 = _____

From the year 2000 we say:
2000 = *two thousand*
2005 = _____ *and five*

3 Take it in turns to say the dates.
10/12/89
the tenth of December, nineteen eighty-nine

1 15/6/06   3 30/10/91
2 3/5/08   4 22/2/04

Hot Tip!
In English we use the past simple of *be* + *born* to talk about dates and places of birth.

*Sara **was born** in winter.
When **were** you **born**?*

PT Grammar
----▶ *be* – Past simple p. 63

3

Past time expressions

Write the time expressions in the correct chronological order.

> 5 years ago   last month
> last week   last year   yesterday

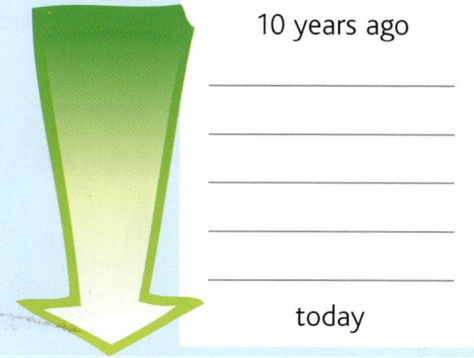

10 years ago
_____
_____
_____
_____
_____
today

Look at the time expressions above and complete the rule.
Besides *yesterday*, or a date, we can use _____ and _____ with *days, weeks, months, years.*
How do you say these in your language?

4 Write 3 sentences about yourself using the past simple of *be* and time expressions.

*Yesterday I wasn't at school.
10 years ago I was a baby.*

5 Complete with your date of birth.
I was born _____ years ago on _____
_____.

Hot Tip!
Be careful! We say *yesterday morning, yesterday afternoon, yesterday evening,* and **last** *night*.

3 CURIOSITY CORNER

1. Joke Time

What did the tornado say to the sports car?

'Want to go for a spin?'

2. Odd Jobs

Complete the crossword with five jobs that teenagers can do. Then use the letters in the red squares to answer the following question.

What is the female equivalent of 'paperboy'?

_ _ _ _ _ _ _ _ _

Pocket money

Teenagers in the UK do lots of odd jobs to earn pocket money. They help around the house, do paper rounds, clean cars, babysit, walk dogs, cut the grass.

Teenagers aged 13 or 14 can do a Saturday job but they must not work for more than five hours a day. Saturday jobs can be in a clothes shop, a music shop, a supermarket etc.

How do they spend their money?

Both girls and boys spend a lot of their pocket money on sweets and chocolate. Girls also buy clothes, shoes, magazines and make-up. Boys prefer to spend their money on computer games, videos and CDs.

What about you?

Do you do odd jobs?
Do you earn pocket money?
What do you most like to spend your money on?

Imagine you see a pair of expensive trainers in a shop.
Do you...
a) ask for them as a birthday or Christmas present?
b) ask your parents again and again until they buy them for you?
c) offer to do odd jobs around the house to earn the money?

CURIOSITY CORNER 3

3 Did you know?

The Empire State Building in New York City gets struck by lightning about 500 times a year!

4 General Knowledge Quiz

Test your general knowledge with this short quiz. Match the questions with the answers.

1 ☐ Who was the first man on the moon?
2 ☐ Which country was the winner of the FIFA World Cup in 2006?
3 ☐ What was the name of the ship in the accident with an iceberg on April 15th, 1912?
4 ☐ Where was Robbie Williams born?
5 ☐ What nationality was Mozart?

A Austrian
B Stoke-on-Trent
C Neil Armstrong
D Italy
E The Titanic

5 Weather Sayings

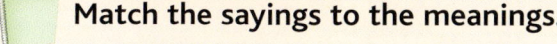 Match the sayings to the meanings.

1 ☐ 'It's raining cats and dogs!'
2 ☐ 'Every cloud has a silver lining.'
3 ☐ 'I'm on cloud nine.'
4 ☐ 'You're making a storm in a teacup.'
5 ☐ 'I'm feeling under the weather.'

A I'm very happy.
B To make a small problem seem greater than it is.
C I'm feeling ill.
D Every difficult situation has a positive side.
E It's raining very heavily.

It's raining cats and dogs!

6 Cool Thought

"It takes a great deal of courage to stand up to your enemies, but even more to stand up to your friends."

J.K. Rowling
(author Harry Potter Series)

twenty-nine 29

Check Your Progress

Units 1-3

1 Reorder the letters to make an adverb of manner.

Lucy is running really KQYULCI *quickly*.

1 Richard is talking really DLYLUO _____.
2 Sam is working really MSCULIYL _____ this evening.
3 Laura always does the washing up really LYLFUCAER _____.
4 They're studying in the library. They're speaking EQLUYTI _____

___ / 4

2 What's the weather like?

In Britain, it's 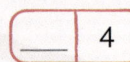 *cloudy* today.
1 In France, it's _____ today.
2 In Spain, it's _____ today.
3 In Denmark, it's 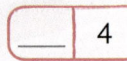 _____ today.
4 In Italy, it's _____ today.

___ / 4

3 Write the verbs in the *-ing* form.

drive — *driving*
1 hang around _____
2 sit _____
3 step _____
4 take _____
5 turn _____
6 wait _____
7 waste _____
8 put _____

___ / 8

4 Use these words to write sentences about Peter's likes and dislikes.

> basketball   do   go   hate   play
> karate   like   love   swimming

1 _____

2 _____

3 _____

___ / 6

5 Find six jobs in the wordsnake.

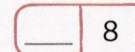

___ / 6

30 thirty

Units 1-3

6 Look at the pictures and write what these people are doing.

He is watching TV.

1 _____

2 _____

3 _____

4 _____

5 _____

6 _____

___ / 6

7 Look at the identity cards and write a sentence about each student.

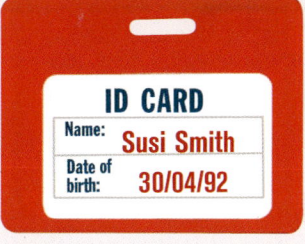
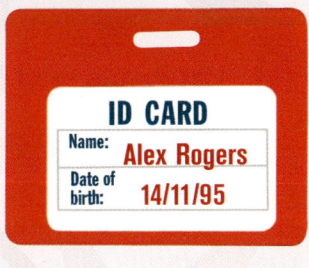

Susi was born on 30th April. She was born in spring.

1 _____
_____
_____

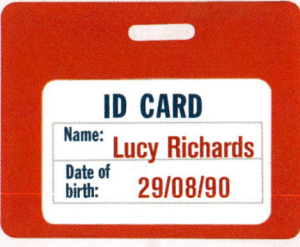

2 _____
_____
_____

3 _____
_____
_____

___ / 6

8 Complete the conversation with the correct form of the past simple of *be*.

Ellie: Where (1) _____ Jane yesterday?
Stephen: She (2) _____ at her grandma's house.
Ellie: (3) _____ you with her?
Stephen: No, I (4) _____. I (5) _____ at a pizza restaurant with my sister. We (6) _____ really hungry.
Ellie: The new pizza restaurant in town? I (7) _____ there on Tuesday. There (8 not/be) _____ many people.
Stephen: And where (9) _____ you yesterday?
Ellie: I (10) _____ at the cinema with Mark.

___ / 10

My final score is: ___ / 50

4 We stayed up late!

1 Listen and read.

We walked for miles!

Jack: This is exciting! David, do you remember when we visited uncle Paul last year?
David: Oh yes, in the north. That was fun!
Sara: Hey, I wasn't there! What did you do?
Jack: Well, now he lives in the city, but last year he lived in the countryside. It was very far, and we didn't have a camper van, so we travelled by train.
David: It was a very slow train, and it stopped everywhere!
Jack: Yeah, then we walked for miles!
David: And I carried the big suitcase. It was so heavy!
Jack: But we weren't very tired – that first night we stayed up late and played cards. It was great!
David: Yeah, uncle Paul is great! He's an artist. He painted a picture of Emi.
Sara: I'm sorry I missed that trip!
Jack: We're nearly there now – look, I can see the Eiffel Tower!

Comprehension

2 Read the following sentences and tick (✓) T (True), F (False) or DS (Doesn't Say).

1 David remembers visiting uncle Paul last year.
2 Sara also visited him.
3 Uncle Paul lives in the countryside.
4 The train often stopped on the journey.
5 David was tired after carrying the suitcases.
6 Uncle Paul was born in autumn.

Vocabulary

 3 Look at the pictures and complete the sentences. Then listen and check.

> ~~in the countryside~~ cards
> by train   a museum
> a picture   a big suitcase

He lived *in the countryside.*

1 She travelled _____

2 We played _____

3 He painted _____

4 I carried _____

5 They visited _____

Sounds Good!

 4 Listen and put the verbs in the correct column.

> ~~asked~~   ~~chatted~~   danced
> ~~called~~   painted   played
> stopped   visited   watched

Group 1 /d/	Group 2 /t/	Group 3 /ɪd/
called	asked	chatted
_____	_____	_____
_____	_____	_____
_____	_____	_____

 5 Listen and check.

Communication

Look & Use

We **visited** uncle Paul last year.
We **travelled** by train.
We **played** cards.

6 Create an imaginary holiday. Then tell your partner about your trip.

I travelled by car.
I visited…

4

1 Listen and read.

Did Mrs Doyle like Paris?

David: There's Sophie!
Sophie: *Salut!* It's great to see you! You arrived very quickly.
Sara: Yes, we didn't stop on the way – we were so excited!
Sophie: Where's Mrs Doyle?
David: She's walking around the city. Did you know that she visited Paris when she was young?
Sophie: Really? Did she study here?
David: I don't think so.
Jack: What did she do? Who did she travel with? Where did she stay?
David: Hey, all these questions! I have no idea! We asked her, but she didn't want to tell us.
Sara: Hush! Mrs Doyle's coming!
Jack: Mrs Doyle! Did you visit Paris when you were young?
Mrs Doyle: Yes, I did!
Sophie: Did you like it?
Mrs Doyle: Like it? I loved it!
Jack: Did you learn any French?
Mrs Doyle: *Mais oui! Est-ce que vous voulez une tasse de thé?*
Jack: No, Mrs Doyle, no more tea!

> *Est-ce que vous voulez une tasse de thé?* (French): Would you like a cup of tea?

Comprehension

2 Circle the correct short answer.

Did they stop on the way to France?
Yes, they did. / **No, they didn't.**

1 Did Sophie know that Mrs Doyle visited Paris when she was young?
Yes, she did. / No, she didn't.

2 Did Mrs Doyle like Paris?
Yes, she did. / No, she didn't.

3 Did she learn any French?
Yes, she did. / No, she didn't.

4 Do they want any tea?
Yes, they do. / No, they don't.

4

Vocabulary

3 Complete the sentences with the correct verbs. Then match them to the pictures.

> talked   danced   called   asked
> studied   ~~watched~~

1 Last night I _watched_ my favourite programme on TV.
2 The disco was great - we _____ all night!
3 Where were you? I _____ your house at eight o'clock.
4 Mr Smith _____ Italian at university.
5 John _____ to a very nice girl at the party yesterday evening.
6 Michelle's mother _____ her to go to the supermarket.

A   B

C   D

E   F

 4 Listen and check.

C 1.26

Communication

Look & Use

Did you **visit** Paris?
Yes, I **did**!
Did she **study** here?
No, she **didn't**.
What **did** she **do**?
She **didn't want** to tell us.

 5 Listen to the conversations and tick (✓) the correct pictures. Then ask and answer questions in pairs.

C 1.27

A *Did Emily watch TV last night?*
B *No, she didn't. She talked to Jamie on the phone.*

My Turn

6 What did you do last night? Write three sentences.

7 Work in pairs. Ask questions to find out what your partner did last night. Then swap roles.

A *Did you study yesterday evening?*
B *Yes, I did. / No, I didn't.*

thirty-five **35**

4 Grammar Focus

Past simple – Regular verbs
Affirmative form

Read the examples.
I carr**ied** the big suitcase.
You arriv**ed** very quickly.
He liv**ed** in the countryside.
She visit**ed** Paris.
It stop**ped** everywhere.
We stay**ed** up all night.
You play**ed** cards.
They travel**led** by train.

Look at the examples again and answer the questions.

What do we add to the base form to make the past simple of regular verbs? ____

Is the past simple form the same for all persons? ____

Past simple – Regular verbs
Spelling

Look at the examples and complete the rules.

| visit → visit**ed** | paint → paint**ed** |

To make the past simple of regular verbs we generally add ____ to the _____ form.

| live → liv**ed** | like → lik**ed** |

When a verb ends in ____ we add ____.

| stop → stop**ped** | fit → fit**ted** |

When a one-syllable verb ends in a single vowel + single consonant we double the _____ and add -ed.

| pre**fer** → prefer**red** |

When a verb ends in a single vowel + a single consonant we double the consonant if it has two syllables and the second one is stressed.

| play → play**ed** | stay → stay**ed** |

When a verb ends in a vowel + ____ we add ____.

| carry → carr**ied** | study → stud**ied** |

When a verb ends in a consonant + y we change the y to ____ and add ____.

1 Put the verbs in brackets in the past simple to complete David's diary.

20

Yesterday I _studied_ (study) in the morning. Then my friend John (1) _____ (call) me and (2) _____ (ask) me to spend the afternoon with him. It (3) _____ (be) great fun!
We (4) _____ (play) football in the park, then (5) _____ (rent) a DVD. We (6) _____ (watch) 'The Incredibles'. Then we (7) _____ (switch) on the computer and (8) _____ (surf) the Internet for half an hour.
Later we (9) _____ (decide) to go to a disco. We (10) _____ (dance) all night. A very cute girl (11) _____ (smile) at me! I really (12) _____ (enjoy) my last day at home.

Tomorrow – Paris!!!

4

PT Grammar
----> Past simple – Regular verbs
pp. 65-70

Past simple
Negative form

Read the examples, then complete the pattern.

José studied last night. Sophie **didn't study** last night.

Emi wagged her tail in France. She **didn't wag** her tail on the journey.

We stopped everywhere. They **didn't stop** on the way.

In the negative form of the past simple the sentence pattern is:

subject + did not (didn't) + _____ _____ of the verb.

2 The following sentences are false. Rewrite them to make them true.

Dinosaurs walked the earth one thousand years ago. (one million years ago)

Dinosaurs didn't walk the earth one thousand years ago. They walked the earth one million years ago.

1 Napoleon lived in England. (in France)
   _____
   _____

2 Zidane played football for Italy. (for France)
   _____
   _____

3 Einstein studied Music. (Physics)
   _____
   _____

4 Romeo loved Beatrice. (Juliet)
   _____
   _____

Past simple
Questions and short answers

Read the examples, then complete the rules.

Did you **do** your homework on Saturday?
No, I **didn't**. / Yes, I **did**.

Did Lucy **like** Paris?
No, she **didn't**. / Yes, she **did**.

Did they **stop** on the way to France?
Yes, they **did**. / No, they **didn't**.

In **questions** the sentence pattern is:

_____ + subject + _____ _____ of the verb.

We use the auxiliary verb _____ for all persons.

In **short answers** the sentence pattern is:

Yes, + subject + _____.
No, + _____ + didn't.

What did Mrs Doyle do in Paris?
Where did she stay?
Who did you see?

Wh- words go _____ the auxiliary verb did.

3 Write the questions in the past simple and give short answers.

you / tidy your bedroom / yesterday? (✓)
A *Did you tidy your bedroom yesterday?*
B *Yes, I did.*

1 he / walk to school / this morning? (✗)
2 they / play computer games / yesterday afternoon? (✓)
3 she / watch a film on TV / last night? (✓)
4 Tom and Pete / play football / last Saturday? (✗)

thirty-seven **37**

4

Ewan McGregor is a Scottish actor. He was born on 31st March 1971 in Crieff, Scotland.

Reading

1 Read the interview with Ewan McGregor. Write the questions in the correct places.

A What did you do in 2004?
B What was your favourite subject at school?
C What did you do in 2007?
D How many countries did you visit?
E Did you train for the trip?

1 _____

'When I was a teenager my favourite subject at school was drama. In 1988 I attended the Guildhall School of Music and Drama where I studied drama for 3 years.'

2 _____

'In 2004 I started a marathon motorcycle trip with my best friend Charley Boorman and a cameraman called Claudio Von Planta. The journey started in April and finished in July. We travelled from London to New York on motorbikes! Lots of people watched the trip on a TV documentary series called Long Way Round.'

3 _____

'Oh, yes! The team studied Russian and practised survival training. We also learned about medical treatment. I needed medical treatment when I crashed my bike into a river in Mongolia!'

4 _____

'We travelled a total distance of 18,887 miles (30,395km) and visited 12 countries. We often stayed in hotels but sometimes we stayed in tents. It was a great adventure!
During the journey we teamed up with UNICEF for charity events. We raised money for various projects including an orphanage in Ukraine. We also visited lots of famous places, for example Mount Rushmore in the USA.'

5 _____

'In 2007 the Long Way Round team decided to get together again for another motorcycle trip! This time we travelled from Scotland to South Africa. We called the journey Long Way Down. It started in May and finished in August 2007.'

2 Answer the questions.

1 Where is Ewan McGregor from?
2 When was he born?
3 Who is his best friend?
4 How many months did the Long Way Round journey last?
5 What famous place did he visit in the USA?

Speaking

3 Work in pairs. Imagine you travelled from Scotland to South Africa. Do some research on the countries you visited, then ask and answer questions. Student A: take the role of a journalist. Student B: take the role of the traveller. Then swap roles.

A Say hello and welcome the interviewee.
B Thank the journalist.
A Ask when the *Long Way Down* journey started.
B Answer.
A Ask who he / she travelled with.
B Answer.
A Ask where he / she stayed.
B Answer.
A Ask what he / she liked about the journey.
B Answer.

Writing

4 Imagine you are back from an incredible journey. Write a paragraph about your experiences.

Describe:
- how you travelled
- which places you visited
- who you travelled with
- what you liked

I started in...
_____
_____
_____
_____

Listening

5 Listen to the interview with a historian about Princess Diana and tick (✓) the correct answers.

INTERVIEW

1 Princess Diana was born on
   A 21st July 1961
   B 1st August 1962
   C 1st July 1961

2 She died
   A in Paris in 1997
   B in London in 1997
   C in Rome in 1997

3 When she finished school she worked as
   A an actress
   B a nanny
   C a doctor

4 She worked with charities and visited
   A hospitals
   B museums
   C castles

5 In 2007 her sons organised
   A a party at Buckingham Palace
   B a dinner with their dad, Prince Charles
   C a concert at Wembley Stadium

5 I didn't bring my camera!

1 Listen and read.

The gladiators fought here

Mrs Doyle: Ah, I love Rome! I visited Rome when I was 18. I went to the Spanish Steps and I threw a coin into the Trevi Fountain. I also saw the Pope at St Peter's! I had a wonderful trip!

Sara: Yeah, it's fantastic here! Let's take some photos!

Mrs Doyle: Oh no, I didn't bring my camera! I left it in the camper van.

Sara: Don't worry, I brought mine.

Jack: I didn't know that there were animal shows here in Roman times.

Sara: What are you reading, Jack?

Jack: My guidebook. I bought it in Paris.

David: Tell us about the gladiators...

Jack: Well, the gladiators fought here.

Francesco: Yes, a lot of gladiators died in the fights. The Emperor didn't miss the fights. He watched and when he gave a 'thumbs up' sign it meant the gladiator lived. A 'thumbs down' sign meant the gladiator died!

Jack: Wow! How awful!

Sara: Hey, come on boys! Let's go and buy some souvenirs.

Jack: Souvenirs? No, I want to take a photo of one of those gladiators over there!

Comprehension

2 Choose the correct alternative to complete the sentences.

Mrs Doyle saw _the Pope_ when she was 18.

  A a gladiator   **B** an Emperor   **C** the Pope

1 Mrs Doyle didn't bring her _____.

  A guidebook   **B** souvenirs   **C** camera

2 In Roman times, gladiators _____ in the Coliseum.

  A played   **B** fought   **C** danced

3 The Emperor _____ missed the gladiator fights.

  A often   **B** sometimes   **C** never

4 Jack wants to _____.

  A take a photo   **B** buy souvenirs   **C** buy a camera

Vocabulary

3 Match the phrases to the pictures. Then listen and check. (C 1.30)

take a photo
buy a souvenir
go sightseeing
buy a guidebook or a map
~~send a postcard~~
go back to the hostel

send a postcard

1 _____
2 _____
3 _____
4 _____
5 _____

4 Match the verbs in exercise 3 with their past form.

1 _____ - sent
2 _____ - took
3 _____ - went (*in 2 phrases*)
4 _____ - bought (*in 2 phrases*)

Communication

Look & Use

I **left** it in the camper van.
I **bought** it in Paris.
I **didn't bring** my camera.

5 Say what Alex did (✓) or didn't do (✗) last Sunday.

~~got up at 8.00~~ (✓)
had tea and toast (✗)
made a cake for his dad (✓)
had lunch with his grandmother (✓)
went to the cinema (✗)
swam for 40 minutes (✗)

Last Sunday Alex got up early, at 8…

My Turn

6 Write six sentences about what you did last weekend. Make sure two sentences are not true!

7 Work with your partner. Tell him / her what you did last weekend and see if he / she can guess which sentences are not true! Then swap roles.

A *Last weekend I went shopping with my friend.*

B *That's true!*

A *Last weekend I sang a song with Robbie Williams.*

B *That's not true! You didn't sing a song with Robbie Williams.*

5

C 1.31 / S 14

1 Listen and read.

Did you bring the sandwiches?

Jack: Hey Sara, did you bring the sandwiches?
Sara: No, I didn't. Oh no, did we forget them?
Mrs Doyle: Don't worry! I brought them. There's a sandwich for everyone. Now, what would you like... cheese, ham, tuna...?
Jack: Cheese, please!
Paolo: So, did you like St Peter's, Sara?
Sara: Oh yes, I did. It's a beautiful church!
Paolo: Did you see Michelangelo's sculpture?
Sara: The *Pietà*? Yes, I did. It's amazing!
Jack: It said in my guidebook that Michelangelo finished it when he was 24. That's really young!
Paolo: Yes, he was very clever. He also designed St Peter's dome and he painted the ceiling in the Sistine Chapel. He was Italian, you know!
Sara: Yeah, yeah, we know!
Paolo: And he also painted a self-portrait in the Sistine Chapel.
Sara: Really?!
Mrs Doyle: Oh, I do love Rome! There are so many fantastic statues and museums and art galleries and...

Hot Tip!

When you want to place particular emphasis on something, you can use the auxiliary verbs *do* and *did* in the affirmative form.
I **do** love Rome! (Present)
I **did** love him. (Past)

Comprehension

2 Read and match the sentences.

Sara didn't
1 Sara liked
2 Michelangelo didn't finish
3 Michelangelo was
4 Michelangelo designed St Peter's
5 Mrs Doyle

A loves Rome.
B the *Pietà* when he was 35.
C bring the sandwiches.
D very clever.
E St Peter's.
F dome and he painted a self-portrait.

5

Vocabulary

 3 Match the words to the pictures. Then listen and check.

- [ ] **A** statue
- [ ] **B** fountain
- [1] **C** church
- [ ] **D** art gallery
- [ ] **E** sculpture
- [ ] **F** castle
- [ ] **G** museum

Communication

Look & Use

Did you **like** St Peter's?
Yes, I **did**.

Did you **bring** the sandwiches?
No, I **didn't**.

 4 Complete the telephone conversation with Sara's answers. Then listen and check.

> ~~Yes Mum, it's beautiful here!~~
> Yes, the *Pietà* is amazing!
> No, we didn't. Maybe tomorrow.
> Yes, we did. The Vatican was wonderful!
> Yes, of course I did!
> OK Mum!
> Ah, you mean the Trevi Fountain?

Sara's mum: Hello Sara. Are you having a good time?
Sara: *Yes Mum, it's beautiful here!*
Sara's mum: Did you go to the Vatican today?
Sara: (1) _____
Sara's mum: Did you see Michelangelo's sculpture... the *Pietà*?
Sara: (2) _____
Sara's mum: And did you see that fountain - oh, what's its name?
Sara: (3) _____
Sara's mum: Yes, that's right.
Sara: (4) _____
Sara's mum: OK. Well, don't forget to throw a coin in and make a wish!
Sara: (5) _____
Sara's mum: Did you send us a postcard?
Sara: (6) _____

Sounds Good!

 5 Listen to the intonation in these questions. Then repeat.

Where did you go on Sunday?
Did you go to the park?
Did you see Amy and Pete?

 6 Now say these questions. Work with a partner. Then listen and check.

Where did you go on Saturday?
Did you go to the cinema?
Who did you go with?

My Turn

7 Work in pairs. Choose a destination from the box. Imagine you are back from a holiday in this city. Go to page 120. Ask and answer questions. Then swap roles.

> London   Rome   New York   Paris

forty-three 43

5 Grammar Focus

Past simple - Irregular verbs

Affirmative form

Many common verbs have an **irregular past form** (see the list of irregular verbs on the inside cover of your *Personal Toolkit*).

It is the same for all persons.

Read the examples.

I **went** to the Spanish Steps.
I **threw** a coin into the Trevi Fountain.

Went is the past simple of **go**.
Threw is the past simple of **throw**.

Find the past simple of these irregular verbs in the dialogue on page 40. Write them in the table.

Base form	Past simple
go	went
bring	_____
see	_____
buy	_____
fight	_____
have	_____
leave	_____

Find the base form of these past simple irregular verbs in the texts on pages 41 and 42. Write them in the table.

Base form	Past simple
_____	swam
_____	made
_____	got up
_____	forgot
_____	sang

Hot Tip!

Some verbs have both a regular and an irregular past simple: *learn* – *learn**ed** / learn**t***

For some verbs the base form and the past simple have the same spelling and pronunciation: **put** – **put**.

For some verbs the base form and the past simple have the same spelling but different pronunciation: **read** /riːd/ – **read** /red/.

1 Find the past simple of these irregular verbs. If you don't know the form, look it up in your Personal Toolkit. Write a sentence with each one and include a past time expression.

go   pay   swim   sleep
meet   ~~wear~~   tell   eat

I wore a blue T-shirt and jeans on Saturday.

2 Complete Sara's postcard with the past simple of the verbs in brackets and the past time expressions in the box.

evening   yesterday   morning

Dear Mum and Dad,
Hi! We **arrived** (arrive) in Rome (1) _____ afternoon and we (2) _____ (meet) Paolo and Francesco at the railway station. We (3) _____ (go) to the Coliseum this (4) _____ and Jack (5) _____ (tell) us lots of information from his guidebook! Yesterday (6) _____, we (7) _____ (have) dinner at Paolo and Francesco's house. We (8) _____ (eat) pasta with tomato sauce!

Ciao! Sara

Mr and Mrs J Smith
14 Park Road
Harrow HA1 4ED
UK

Past simple - Irregular verbs

Negative form

Read the examples, then complete the pattern.

I **didn't** bring my camera!

I **didn't** know that there were animal shows here.

The Emperor **didn't** miss the fights.

In the **negative form** the sentence pattern is:
subject + _____ + base form of the irregular verb.

We use the auxiliary verb *didn't* for all persons.

Questions and short answers

Read the examples, then complete the rules.

Did you bring the sandwiches? **Yes, I did.**

Did she forget the sandwiches?
No, she didn't.

Did you see Michelangelo's sculpture?
No, I didn't.

In **questions** the sentence pattern is:
_____ + subject + _____ _____ of the verb.

We use the auxiliary verb _____ for all persons.

In **short answers** the sentence pattern is:
Yes, + _____ + did.
_____, + subject + didn't.

The answers to *Wh-* questions (with *What, Where, When, How,* etc.) always give specific information.

A **What** did you do on Saturday?
B *I went to the cinema.*

A **When** did you meet Shakira?
B *I met her last week!*

PT Grammar
→ Past simple – Irregular verbs pp. 67-70

5

3 Write negative sentences.

I went to the cinema last weekend.
I didn't go to the cinema last weekend.

1 She took a lot of photos on holiday.
   _____

2 We made a cake yesterday afternoon.
   _____

3 They wrote a letter to the President.
   _____

4 Write questions and short answers.

you / go / to party / Sunday / ? (✓)
A *Did you go to the party on Sunday?*
B *Yes, I did.*

1 she / fly / to New York / last week / ? (✗)
A _____
B _____

2 they / meet / Anastacia / at the concert / ? (✗)
A _____
B _____

3 your brother / learn / Spanish / at school / ? (✓)
A _____
B _____

5 Complete Annie's e-mail with the correct form of the verbs in the box.

have   do   buy   see   ~~go~~   meet

Hi Helen!
I _went_ to London last weekend with my mum and dad. On Saturday morning we went on the London Eye and we (1) _____ all the sights from the sky! Then we (2) _____ a picnic in Hyde Park and we (3) _____ some souvenirs. On Sunday we went to Buckingham Palace but we (4) _____ _____ the Queen!
What did you (5) _____ last weekend?
Bye,
Annie

CLIL Discovering Food

Food from Afar

1 Match the words to the photos.

1. ☐ cocoa (chocolate)
2. ☐ pumpkin
3. ☐ beans
4. ☐ pineapples
5. ☐ vanilla
6. ☐ peanuts
7. ☐ sunflower
8. ☐ potatoes
9. ☐ avocados
10. [A] sweetcorn
11. ☐ chilli peppers
12. ☐ tomatoes

2 Play the Memory Game. Look at the food for thirty seconds and then close your books. Work in pairs and check how many exotic foods you can remember.

 **3** Do you know where pumpkins and pineapples are originally from? Discuss in pairs. Then listen and read the text to check your answer.

People believe that the Italian born explorer first went to sea when he was only ten years old. His first voyage, in search of new trading routes between Europe and India, was in 1492. Christopher Columbus left Spain and sailed west with three ships, *Santa Maria*, *Pinta* and *Niña*. After five weeks he arrived at the Bahamas. He thought it was India, but he actually discovered the new continent America. On the next trip he made, he took seventeen ships, bringing back lots more exotic foods. Pumpkins, for instance, coming from Mexico, and pineapples from the Caribbean.

4 Read the text again and answer the questions.

Where was Christopher Columbus from?
He was Italian.

1. When did Columbus first go to sea?
2. What were the names of the ships Columbus took for his first voyage?
3. Which islands did he discover in 1492?
4. How many ships did he take on his second trip?

Project Time

Find out where these foods are originally from. Then report to the class.

banana   sugar   pepper   coconut

How is Chocolate Produced?

1 Work in pairs. Think of how we use chocolate.

You can use chocolate for… hot chocolate.

 2 Read the information card and complete the sentences. Then listen and check.

Chocolate is made from cocoa whose scientific name is *Theobroma*, a __Greek__ word. Chocolate comes from (1) _____ Africa, (2) _____ and (3) _____ America and (4) _____ Countries. It is full of (5) _____ for example (6) _____ and (7) _____. It is also good for you because it gives you (8) _____.

CHOCOLATE INFORMATION CARD

Derivation:	Fruit of the cocoa tree. (pod, seeds, white pulp)
Scientific Name:	*Theobroma* = 'food for the gods' in Greek.
Origins:	West Africa (Ivory Coast, Nigeria, Uganda, Tanzania, Cameroon) Central and South America (Mexico, Brazil, Colombia, Ecuador), Eastern Countries (Malaysia, Papua New Guinea).
Medicinal Properties:	Cocoa and chocolate are full of minerals, including magnesium and iron. It has anti-oxidant (anti-ageing) properties. It gives you energy and helps you overcome fatigue.

3 Here is how chocolate is made. Look at the photos. They are in the correct order. Using the photos put the phrases into the correct order. The first and last are in the right place.

- [1] Farmers pick the ripe pods in the plantation and open them.
- [ ] They roast the cocoa beans then add sugar.
- [ ] The beans dry in the sun.
- [ ] They melt the beans so they become chocolate concentrate.
- [ ] They heat the mixture twice and pour it into moulds.
- [ ] They send the beans to chocolate factories.
- [7] They wrap the chocolate bars in paper and deliver them to the shops.

Project Time

Work in groups, create a poster about chocolate. Use the information from this page and add any other information you can find out.

6 How far is it to Barcelona?

 1 Listen and read.

How long does it take by plane?

Mrs Doyle: OK! Let's say goodbye to Italy. This is the French border.
Sara: Goodbye Italy… see you again soon!
Jack: How far is it to Barcelona now?
Mrs Doyle: Well, probably about seven hours.
Jack: Seven hours! That's about 13 hours in total from Rome!
Mrs Doyle: Yes, it's a long way in the camper van.
Jack: But, I'm tired… and bored! How long does it take by plane?
David: About two hours, I think.
Jack: Humph… two hours! And how long does it take by ferry?
David: I'm not sure. But probably about 20 hours.
Jack: 20 hours! That's ridiculous!!
Sara: Jack, be quiet!
Jack: How fast can this camper van go?
David: There is another way you can go to Barcelona you know, and it's not boring!
Jack: How?
David: On foot!
Jack: On foot?! But…
Everyone: Ha! Ha! Ha!

Comprehension

2 Answer the questions.

Where are they? *At the French border.*
1 Is it a long way to Barcelona?
2 How long does it take to fly to Barcelona?
3 What takes 20 hours?
4 Does Jack think going to Barcelona by ferry is a good idea?
5 What does David suggest Jack can do?

48 forty-eight

6

Vocabulary

3 Match the words to the pictures. Then listen and check.

~~car~~
bicycle
ferry
motorbike
train
coach
bus
aeroplane

car   1 _____   2 _____

3 _____   4 _____   5 _____

6 _____   7 _____

Communication

Look & Use

How far is it to Barcelona?
How long **does it take** by ferry?
You can go to Barcelona **on foot**.

4 Listen and complete the information. Then ask and answer questions in pairs.

Oxford to Stratford-upon-Avon
By (1) _____
(2) _____ hour and a half

Oxford to Windsor
By (3) _____
(4) _____ hour

Oxford to Alton Towers
By (5) _____
(6) _____ and a half hours

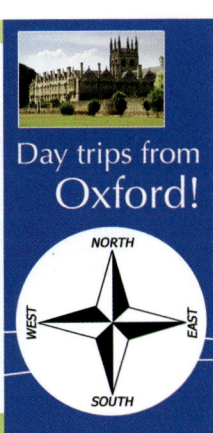

Day trips from Oxford!

A *How long does it take to get from Oxford to Stratford-upon-Avon?*
B *It takes 1 hour and a half by train.*

5 Complete the questions with the adjectives below. Then match the questions to the answers.

~~far~~

tall   long

wide   high

How _far_ is London from York?
1 How _____ is your brother?
2 How _____ is the English Channel?
3 How _____ is the Eiffel Tower?
4 How _____ is the River Thames?

A It's 324 metres.
B It's 344 kilometres.
C He's 1 metre 80 centimetres.
D It's about three hours by train.
E It's about 50 kilometres between Dover and Calais.

My Turn

6 Work in pairs. Use the adjectives in exercise 5 to ask your partner about cities, people and places that you know. Answer his / her questions. Then swap roles.

A *How far is London from Oxford?*
B *It's ... km.*

forty-nine   49

6

 **1** Listen and read.

Is this the right way?

Sara: Wow! Barcelona is beautiful!
Jack: I'm tired...
David: Are you sure this is the right road, Mrs Doyle?
Mrs Doyle: Yes, why?
David: Well, José said to go towards the north of the city, not the south. He lives near Park Güell.
Mrs Doyle: Oh David. Don't be silly! I know where I am.
Sara: No, I think David's right.
Jack: Oh no, now we're lost!
David: OK. OK. Don't panic. Let's ask for directions. Excuse me, can you tell me the way to Park Güell?
Man: Yes, OK, go straight ahead, then turn left and take the second road on the right. Go past the fountain and turn right at the museum.
David: OK. How long does it take to get there?
Man: About 20 minutes.
David: Thank you.
Sara: Can you remember all that, David?
David: I think so. OK, so, go straight ahead and turn right.
Jack: No, David, turn left!

Comprehension

2 Answer the questions.

Who is tired?

Jack

1 Does José live near Park Güell?
2 Does the man tell David to go past the fountain?
3 Does it take ten minutes to get there?
4 Can David remember the directions?

Vocabulary

 3 Match the pictures to the directions. Then listen and check.

> turn left   turn right
> ~~go straight ahead~~
> take the second road on the right
> cross the road

go straight ahead

1 _____

2 _____

3 _____

4 _____

4
 C 1.43

Look at the map. Match the places to the words. Then listen and check.

- [ ] A cinema
- [ ] B library
- [ ] C supermarket
- [ ] D church
- [ ] E school
- [1] F department store
- [ ] G roundabout
- [ ] H bus stop
- [ ] I bank
- [ ] J hospital
- [ ] K police station
- [ ] L restaurant
- [ ] M railway station
- [ ] N traffic lights

Sounds Good!

 C 1.44

5 Listen and repeat the following directions.

Go straight ahead.

Turn right at the roundabout.

Take the second road on the right.

Turn left at the traffic lights.

 C 1.44

6 Listen again and underline the stressed words. Then repeat.

Communication

Look & Use

Excuse me, can you **tell me the way** to Park Güell?
Yes, **go straight ahead**, then turn left and take the second road on the right.

 C 1.45

7 Listen to the mini dialogues and follow the directions on the map in exercise 4.

8 Work in pairs. Look at the map in exercise 4 and take turns to ask and give directions to the following places.

1 hospital   3 bus stop
2 library   4 school

My Turn

9 Work in pairs. Think of a place near your school. Give your partner directions from your school to this place. Your partner tries and guesses what place it is. Then swap roles.

fifty-one 51

6 Grammar Focus

How + adjective

Read the examples, then choose the correct option.

How wide is the River Thames?

How high is Mount Everest?

How old are you?

We use *how* with **adjectives / nouns** to ask questions about specific characteristics (age, dimension, distance, for example).

*It's 16 kilometres **wide**.*

*It's 8,848 metres **high**.*

*I'm 12 years **old**.*

In answers we put the adjective **before / after** measurements.

Read the examples again, then complete the table.

_____	age
How tall...?	height
_____	height
How long...?	length
How far...?	distance
_____	width
How deep...?	depth
How heavy...?	weight

1 Complete the sentences with the words in the box.

| heavy | deep | tall | high | far |

1 How _____ is your cousin?
2 How _____ is Barcelona from Rome?
3 How _____ is the Atlantic Ocean?
4 How _____ is Mount Fiji?
5 How _____ is an elephant?

2 Write the question for each answer.

1 _____
It's about 1,715 km from London to Madrid.

2 _____
My grandmother is 88!

3 _____
The lake is 150 metres deep. Be careful!

4 _____
My apartment block is 100 metres high!

Hot Tip!

How long does it take by plane?
It takes about two hours.

We can use **How long** to ask questions about duration.

Asking for directions

When we want to know **where** a place is, we can simply ask:

Where is ... please?

When we want to ask for **directions** we can say:

Can you tell me the way to... ?

Can you tell me where... is?

Is this the right road for... ?

3 Write questions.

can / way / the railway station
1 _____?

can / where / the cinema
2 _____?

is / right / the police station
3 _____?

can / tell / where / the bank
4 _____?

6

PT Grammar
- *How* + adjective p. 32
- Prepositions of movement p. 43
- The imperative pp. 44-45
- Means of transport p. 55

Giving directions

Read the examples, then complete the rule.

Turn left at the roundabout.
Go straight ahead.
Take the second road on the right.

We use the **imperative** to give directions. We form the imperative with the base _____ of the verb.
We do not use a subject pronoun.

Underline the directions in the dialogue on page 50, then complete the table.

past the cinema   the third road on the right
left   ~~straight ahead~~   right

go	turn	take
straight ahead	_____	_____
_____		

Prepositions of movement

Look at the pictures and read the directions.

Go **along** this street.

Go **past** the cinema.

Go **down** the hill.

Go **into** the park.

How do you say these prepositions in your language?

Underline the prepositions of movement in these sentences.

A boy is walking towards the cinema.
A red car is going up the hill.
There's a bridge over the river.
Go across that road then turn left.
Go through the tunnel.
There's a large car park under the cinema.

Now try and guess their meaning.

 **4** Look at the map and complete the dialogues with prepositions of movement. Then listen and check.

1 **Man:** Excuse me, can you tell me the way to the bank, please?
   Woman: Yes, go _____ Regent Road. Go _____ the cinema and the school. Turn right _____ East Street. The bank is on the right.

2 **Woman:** Excuse me, can you tell me where the library is?
   Man: The library? Yes, go _____ Regent Road. Then turn right and go _____ Market Road. Go _____ the park. The library is on the left.

fifty-three 53

6 CURIOSITY CORNER

1 Did you know?

The Channel Tunnel is the second longest railway tunnel in the world. It is 50,450 km (31.35 miles) long. It took seven years and about 13,000 workers to dig the tunnel! Today you can travel from London to Paris by train in 2 hours 15 minutes.

2 Joke Time

What's black and white and red all over?

A newspaper (red / read)!

3 Incredible!

Heathrow Airport is the biggest airport in Britain and it is one of the busiest airports in the world. Over 64 million people travel to or from Heathrow every year!

4 Post Facts

The traditional British post box is bright red and it first appeared in Britain in the 1850s.
When you post a letter in Britain, you can choose to buy a first class stamp or a second class stamp. First class is the quickest!
Letters and parcels are delivered by the Royal Mail which is the UK's national postal service. The Royal Mail delivers 84 million items every working day!

The 'Penny Black' was the world's first postage stamp.

54 fifty-four

CURIOSITY CORNER 6

5 UK Tourist Attractions

Every year millions of tourists visit the UK. Here are some photos of several top UK tourist attractions. Match the places with the photos.

1. ☐ Canterbury Cathedral
2. ☐ The Eden Project
3. ☐ The Tower of London
4. ☐ Blackpool Pleasure Beach
5. ☐ The London Eye

A B C D E

6 Summer Holidays

Children in the UK have a 6 week summer holiday. In fact, they have the shortest school summer holidays in the European Union.

How long are your school summer holidays?

7 Wordsearch

Find these words in the wordsearch. Then use the remaining letters to find the name of a popular tourist attraction in London.

1. supermarket
2. art gallery
3. fountain
4. bank
5. castle
6. church
7. statue
8. museum
9. sculpture

_ _ _ _ _ _ _ _ _ _ _ _ _ _ _ _

```
T R S C U L P T U R E
A R T G A L L E R Y B
A C A S T L E F A L A
G A T M U S E U M R N
F O U N T A I N S Q K
U A E C H U R C H R E
S U P E R M A R K E T
```

8 Question Time

1. The minimum age for driving a car in the UK is
   - ☐ A 16
   - ☐ B 17
2. In the UK traffic drives on
   - ☐ A the right-hand side of the road.
   - ☐ B the left-hand side of the road.

fifty-five 55

Units 4-6 Check Your Progress

1 Find six past time expressions in the wordsnake.

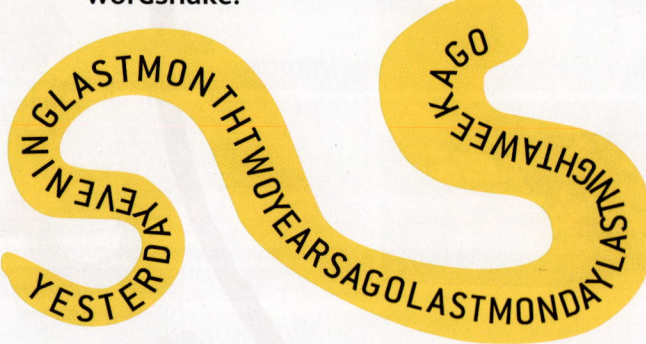

1. _____
2. _____
3. _____
4. _____
5. _____
6. _____

[__] 6

2 Match the words to the definitions.

sculpture — **A** a religious place
1 fountain — **B** a place where you can see lots of paintings
2 church — **C** a figure of a person or an animal
3 art gallery — **D** an object with water coming from it
4 statue — **E** an object made from different types of material

[__] 4

3 Look at the pictures. What did Pippa do when she was on holiday in New York?

1 She took some _____.

2 She bought a _____.

3 She bought a _____.

4 She sent me a _____.

[__] 4

4 Read the definitions and find the type of transport in the wordsearch. Write the word next to the definition.

1 This type of transport can go very fast and you can ride it.

_ _ _ _ _ _ _ _ _

2 This type of transport is long and travels very fast. It doesn't travel on roads.

_ _ _ _ _

3 This type of transport takes you into the air.

_ _ _ _ _ _ _ _ _

4 This type of transport travels on water.

_ _ _ _ _

5 This type of transport can take four or five people on a trip.

_ _ _

```
F E R R Y L E Y T
F G R W D C G H R
W Q F B H K Y H A
E R C G J M V N I
T F A J I F S V N
A E R O P L A N E
F R H T T J U L L
R R D G J N C K K
M O T O R B I K E
```

[__] 5

56 fifty-six

Units 4-6

5 Complete the postcard with the past simple of the verbs.

Dear Susy,
Hello from Edinburgh! I (1) _____ (get up) really early yesterday morning and I (2) _____ (leave) London at 6 o'clock. I (3) _____ (travel) by train and I (4) _____ (arrive) here at about 11 o'clock.
I (5) _____ (go) sightseeing in the afternoon.
I (6) _____ (go) to Edinburgh Castle first and I (7) _____ (buy) a guidebook and some souvenirs at the castle shop. Then I (8) _____ (walk) along the Royal Mile (it's a long street) and I (9) _____ (visit) Holyrood Palace (the Queen's house in Edinburgh). I (10) _____ (see) lots of beautiful paintings and statues. I (11) _____ (take) lots of photos and I (12) _____ (send) some postcards to my friends – this is yours!!
Love Erika

Miss Susy Cook
14 Park Avenue
IG3 9HS
LONDON

___ | 12

6 Make negative (✗) and interrogative (?) sentences in the past simple. Remember to add *Did / didn't*!

1 she / go / to the party / on Friday night (✗)
2 he / do / his homework / last night (?)
3 you / send / an e-mail / this morning (?)
4 Laura and Sara / meet / Philip and John / yesterday. (✗)
5 Jim / pass / his driving test / last week (?)

___ | 5

7 Reorder the words and insert an adjective to make the questions.

long   far   old   deep   high

1 A is / to / Edinburgh / how / it / ?
  B It's three hours by train.
2 A how / is / best / your / friend / ?
  B She's 15.
3 A the / how / North Sea / is / ?
  B It's only about 94 metres.
4 A Mont Blanc / is / how / ?
  B It's 4,807 metres.
5 A how / take / it / to / does / to / Venice / get / ?
  B It takes about four hours by car.

___ | 10

8 Complete the sentences with a preposition of movement.

Go _under_ the bridge.

1 Go _____ the road.

2 Go _____ the cinema.

3 Go _____ the shop.

4 Go _____ the hill.

___ | 4

My final score is: ___ | 50

fifty-seven 57

7 Barcelona is better...

1 Listen and read.

He's taller than José

Jack: I can't wait to see José again. He's such a fantastic guy.

Sara: Yes, he was always more cheerful and more extrovert than everybody else at the Camp.

David: Not like Asim. Do you remember what he was like when he arrived at the Camp? Shyer than everybody.

Jack: But more intelligent! He was brilliant at playing chess and using computers.

Sara: Look! There's José! Over there with the guitar and the brown bag!

Jack: That's not José! He's taller than José.

Sara: OK, I can see him now!

Jack & David: Where?

Sara: Over there, standing near the dragon fountain.

Jack: That's not him! José isn't as thin as that boy.

Sara: OK! OK! I give up!

Emi: Woof! Woof!

Jack: Emi! Don't you start too! That's not José. He's older than José, too.

José: *Hombres!*

All: José!

Jack: Where were you?

José: I'm sorry guys! I was a bit hungry so...

Sara: You went to get some food!

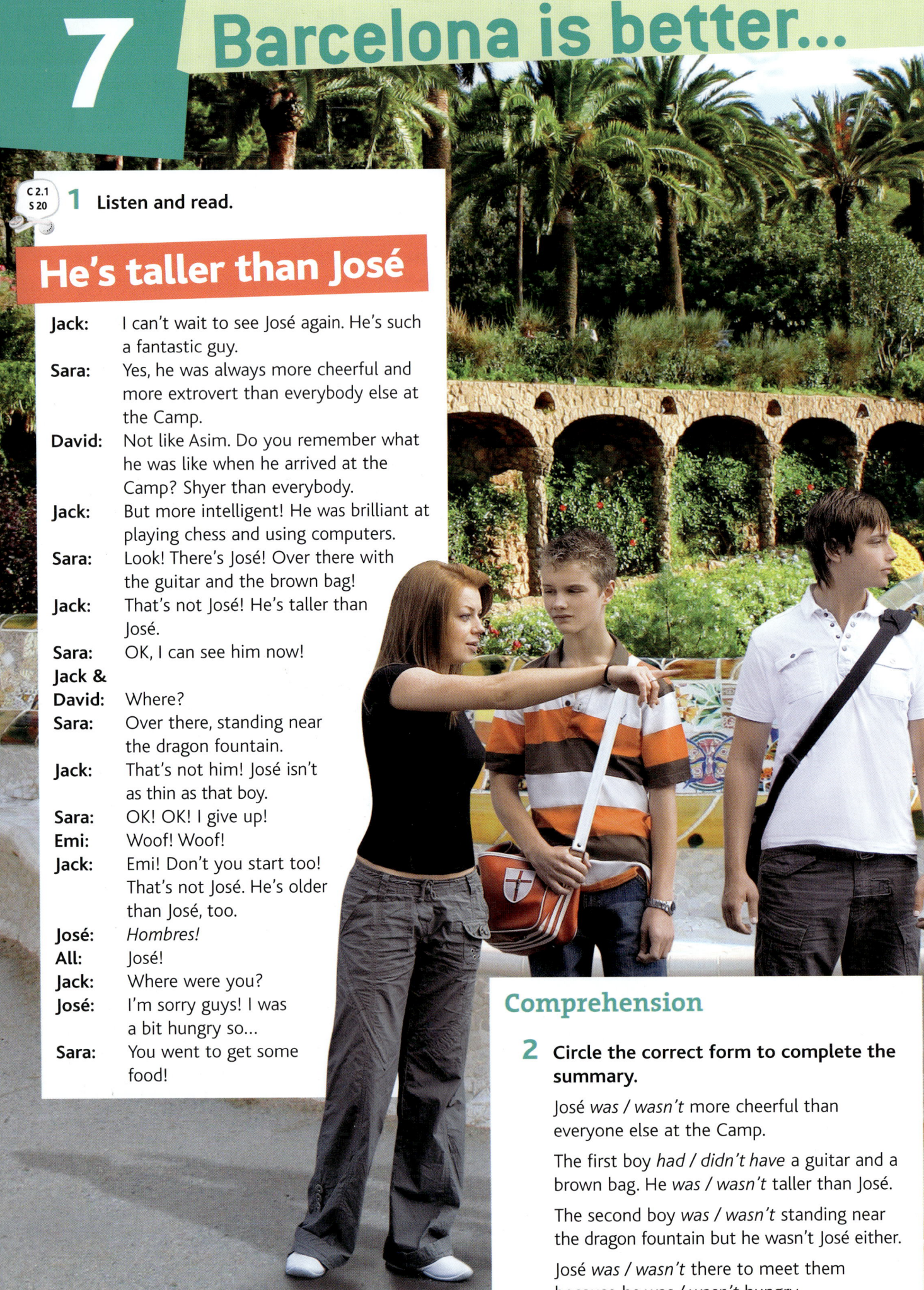

Comprehension

2 Circle the correct form to complete the summary.

José *was / wasn't* more cheerful than everyone else at the Camp.

The first boy *had / didn't have* a guitar and a brown bag. He *was / wasn't* taller than José.

The second boy *was / wasn't* standing near the dragon fountain but he wasn't José either.

José *was / wasn't* there to meet them because he *was / wasn't* hungry.

7

Vocabulary

 3 Match the words to the pictures. Then listen and check.

intelligent   cheerful
extrovert   shy

 1
 2
 3
 4

4 Match the opposites.

sensible	A unfriendly
1 friendly	B calm
2 optimistic	C insensitive
3 sensitive	D impatient
4 moody	E silly
5 patient	F pessimistic

5 Use three adjectives to describe:
1 a friend   3 a relation
2 a teacher   4 a family friend

My friend is John. He's friendly, patient and sensible.

Communication

Look & Use

What's José **like?**
He's cheerful and extrovert.

6 Work in pairs. Ask your partner about the people in exercise 5. Then swap roles.

A *My friend is John.*
B *What's he like?*
A *He's friendly, patient and sensible.*

7 Look at the pictures. Complete the sentences with the words in the box.

tall / taller   old / older   ~~thin~~ / thinner

Anna is as ___thin___ as Paul.
1 Emily is as _____ as Sam.
2 Anna is _____ than the others.
3 Paul is as _____ as Sam.
4 Sam is _____ than Emily.
5 Paul is _____ than Anna.

 8 Listen and check.

My Turn

9 Describe the physical appearance and personality of a classmate. In pairs, take turns to guess the person being described.

He's tall and slim. He's got blue eyes and short brown hair. He's a very friendly person.

7

1 Listen and read.

Which place did you prefer?

José: Well, what do you think about my city, Barcelona?
Jack: Well it's a bit boring.
David: Jack meant beautiful.
José: I heard what he said! He thinks Barcelona is more boring than Paris or Rome!
Sara: Oh, take no notice of Jack! He just thought the girls were prettier in Paris and the shops were better in Rome.
José: Huh! And what do you two think?
Sara: Well, I think the people were friendlier in Rome than they were in Paris.
David: ... and the food was better in Rome but the museums were cheaper in Paris.
José: Well perhaps Barcelona is smaller than Rome or Paris, but the football team is better - and the city is cleaner and safer and of course nearer the sea! Let's take a look at the city.

Comprehension

2 Read the following sentences and tick (✓) T (True) or F (False).

	T	F
Jack said Barcelona was beautiful.	☐	✓
1 Jack thought the girls were prettier in Rome.	☐	☐
2 Sara thought the people in Rome were friendlier than in Paris.	☐	☐
3 David thought the food was better in Paris.	☐	☐
4 David also thought the museums were cheaper in Paris.	☐	☐
5 José thinks Barcelona is cleaner than Paris.	☐	☐

Vocabulary

3 Match the opposites. Then listen and check.

boring — A dirty
1 big — B poor
2 cheap — C expensive
3 clean — D bad
4 fast — E noisy
5 long — F small
6 quiet — G interesting
7 rich — H slow
8 good — I short

60 sixty

Communication

4 Look at the photos. Ask and answer questions in pairs.

A *Which city is more expensive?*

B *I think London is more expensive than New York.*

Look & Use

Barcelona is **more** boring than Paris.
The girls were prett**ier** in Paris.
The food was **better** in Rome.
José isn't **as** thin **as** that boy.

City

more expensive?

Book
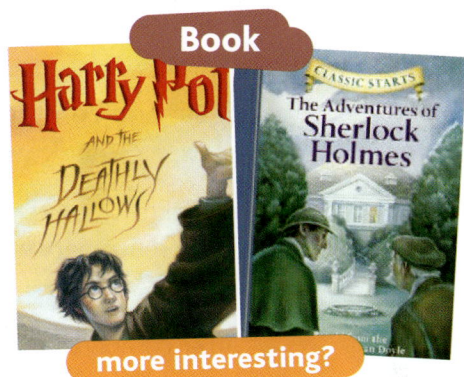
more interesting?

Footballer

more famous?

Sport

more dangerous?

5 Compare your answers with your partner.

A *I think London is **more** expensive **than** New York.*

B *Yes, I agree.*

A *No, I don't agree. I think London is **as** expensive **as** New York.*

Sounds Good!

 C 2.6

6 Listen and repeat these famous sayings. Then in pairs talk about what you think they mean.

As blind as a bat.	As free as a bird.
As busy as a bee.	As light as a feather.
As cold as ice.	As quick as a flash.
As cool as a cucumber.	As slippery as a snake.

My Turn

7 Which do you prefer? Ask and answer in pairs.

> ~~a rock concert / a classical music concert~~
> eating fast food / eating in a restaurant
> English / Science
> reading a book / watching a film
> playing video games / playing tennis

A *Which do you prefer? A rock concert **or** a classical music concert?*

B *I prefer classical concerts **because** they are quieter than rock concerts.*

sixty-one **61**

7 Grammar Focus

Comparatives

Look at the examples. How do you say these sentences in your language?

He's **taller than** José.
She's **more optimistic than** her brother.
The people were **friendlier** in Rome.
The shops were **better** in Rome.

Read the examples again and complete the rules.

We use the _____ form of adjectives to show the difference between two people, objects, or places.

We use _____ after comparative adjectives.

We can also have a comparative adjective without *than*.

Spelling

Read the examples and complete the rules.

Short adjectives	
short	short**er**
cheap	cheap**er**

For adjectives of **one syllable** we generally add *-er*.

thin	thin**ner**
big	big**ger**

For adjectives of **one syllable** ending in consonant + one vowel + consonant we double the consonant and add _____.

late	late**r**
nice	nice**r**

For adjectives of **one syllable** ending in _____ we add _____.

happy	happ**ier**
healthy	health**ier**

For adjectives of **two syllables** ending in consonant + *y* we drop the _____ and add *-ier*.

Long adjectives	
expensive	**more** expensive
boring	**more** boring

For all other adjectives of two or more syllables we use _____ + **adjective**.

Irregular adjectives	
good	**better**
bad	**worse**

Some comparative forms are irregular.

1 Write the comparative form of these adjectives.

easy   *easier*

1 nice _____   4 bad _____
2 wet _____   5 tall _____
3 exciting _____   6 pretty _____

2 Complete the sentences with the comparative form of the adjectives in brackets.

Aeroplanes are *faster* than cars. (fast)

1 Travelling by train is _____ than driving. (relaxing)
2 Walking is _____ than driving. (ecological)
3 The weather in Spain is _____ than in England. (dry)
4 Some means of transport are _____ for the environment than others. (good)
5 Australia is _____ than Italy. (big)

62 sixty-two

PT Grammar
----> Comparatives pp. 24-25

7

3 Look at the pictures, use the prompts, and write sentences. Use the comparative form of the adjectives.

salads / healthy / hamburgers
Salads are healthier than hamburgers.

1 Mike / strong / Jerry
_____
_____

2 cars / expensive / bikes
_____
_____

3 elephants / big / mice
_____
_____

4 English / easy / Chinese
_____
_____

As... as

Read the examples and complete the pattern.

*London is **as expensive as** New York.*

*Footballers are **as rich as** film stars.*

We use the affirmative form of the verb _____ + adjective + **as** to say that people and things are equal.

Read the examples and complete the rules.

*José isn't **as thin as** that boy.*

*A sandwich is not **as expensive as** a pizza.*

We use the negative form of the verb _____ to say that people and things are not equal. The pattern is:

negative verb + **as** + _____ + **as** + noun.

4 Reorder the words and write sentences.

as / sister / my / as / my / brother / is / tall
My sister is as tall as my brother.

1 Rome / as / not / big / Pisa / is / as
_____

2 as / strong / are / lions / as / tigers
_____

3 countryside / noisy / is / the / as / not / city / the / as
_____
_____

4 rich / Henry / as / is / Sonia / as
_____

5 What do you think? Write sentences using *as... as / not as... as*.

lions / tigers (fast)
*Lions are **as fast as** tigers.*
*Lions **aren't as fast as** tigers.*

1 Tom Cruise / Johnny Depp (handsome)
_____

2 action films / romantic films (good)
_____

3 tennis / martial arts (dangerous)
_____

4 geography / English (interesting)
_____

5 Beckham / Kaká (famous)
_____

6 English food / Italian food (delicious)
_____

sixty-three **63**

7 Skills

Listening

 1 **Listen to Lisa and Chris deciding where to go on their family holiday this year. Read the sentences and tick (✓) T (True) or F (False).**

	T	F
They went to the seaside last year.	✓	
1 Lisa thinks visiting a European city is more interesting than the seaside.		
2 The children think playing on the beach is more boring than sightseeing.		
3 Chris thinks travelling by car is worse than travelling by plane.		
4 Lisa thinks travelling by plane is cheaper than travelling by boat.		
5 They decide to travel by train.		

 **2** **Listen and tick (✓) the correct answer.**

1 What's it like?   2 What's he like?   3 What does she like?

A    A    A

B    B    B

C    C    C

64 sixty-four

7

Welcome to Team Up Chat Room

▶ Team Up Chat Room

Room 1 ✕

Chat

Hi there!
My name's Bethan and I'm 13 years old. Bethan's a Welsh name so my friends often call me Beth or Bethy because it's easier to say.
I live in the South of England in a place called Reigate near Gatwick Airport and not far from London. Very handy!
I'm half Welsh and half English because my mum's from Wales and my dad's from England.
I'm tall and slim and I've got very big feet. I suppose I'm quite pretty; I've got long, straight blonde hair and big blue eyes.
I'm very friendly and chatty and I'm never moody. I think I'm quite intelligent and practical too.
In my free time I love playing and watching football and doing any kind of sport. I also like using my PC, visiting chat rooms like this one, playing games and surfing on the Internet. I love all kinds of music and I can play the saxophone. I don't like shopping and make-up but I like to look nice when I go out with my friends.
Bye for now!
Bethan

Reading

3 Read the following entry in a Chat Room and answer the questions.

What nationality is Bethan?
She's half Welsh and half English.

1 Where does she live?
2 What is she like?
3 What does she like?
4 What doesn't she like?

Writing

4 Write a Chat Room entry like Bethan's. Describe your physical appearance and personality. Say what you like and don't like.

Speaking

5 Work in pairs. Compare the two pictures and decide which one you prefer.
You can use these words:

warmer   more interesting
funnier   more boring

A *I think I prefer the first picture because...*

B *I prefer the second picture because...*

sixty-five 65

8 The best holiday ever

1 Listen and read.

Pizza is the best food in the world!

Mrs Doyle: So kids, what is your favourite place so far on this trip?
Jack: The Coliseum with the gladiators was definitely the best thing for me!
Mrs Doyle: It's one of the oldest monuments in the world!
David: It might be the oldest but the highest on our trip was the Eiffel Tower at 325 metres.
Jack: How can you remember that David? You're the worst swot I know!
Mrs Doyle: David has a good memory for details.
Sara: I think the most romantic place was the Trevi Fountain where we threw coins and made a wish!
Jack: Who cares about the most *romantic*! What about the scariest part of the trip – the roads in the centre of Rome!!!
Mrs Doyle: Yes, I agree Jack. They were very scary! Italians are the craziest drivers I know. But what's the best food of all?
Everyone: Pizza!!!

Comprehension

2 Answer the questions.

What was the oldest monument on the trip?
The Coliseum.

1 What was the highest monument they visited?

2 What was the most romantic place they went to?

3 What was the scariest part of the trip?

4 Who were the craziest drivers?

5 What do they think the best food of all is?

Vocabulary

3 Match the words to the pictures. Then listen and check.

- [D] city
- 1 [ ] building
- 2 [ ] mountains
- 3 [ ] river
- 4 [ ] tower
- 5 [ ] lake
- 6 [ ] park
- 7 [ ] woods

Communication

Look & Use

It's one of **the** old**est** monuments **in** the world!
The most romantic place was the Trevi Fountain.

4 Match the two parts of the sentences. Then listen and check.

Ben Nevis is
1 The Shannon is
2 The CN Tower in Canada is
3 Lake Baikal in Russia is
4 Oslo is

A the most expensive city in the world.
B the highest mountain in Britain.
C the longest river in Ireland.
D the deepest lake in the world.
E the tallest tower in the world.

5 Work in pairs. Take turns to ask and answer questions.

~~oldest~~   highest   longest   smallest   most dangerous

old / building in London?
A *What is the oldest building in London?*
B *I think it's the Tower of London.*

1 long / river in the world?
2 high / mountain in Europe?
3 dangerous / creature in the world?
4 small / country in the world?

My Turn

6 Work in pairs. Write a quiz about your country. Write five questions, then exchange your quiz with another group.

A *What's the most famous opera house in…?*
B *It's…*
A *What's the oldest monument in…?*
B *We think it's…*

8

1 Listen and read.

Yours is just as nice as hers

Sara:	That was the best holiday ever!
David:	Yes, it was great! Did you buy any presents?
Sara:	Yes! Look at what I bought for my parents.
David:	A miniature Eiffel Tower!
Sara:	Yes, it's the smallest I found.
David:	I got one too! But yours is smaller than mine.
Mrs Doyle:	Don't worry David, yours is just as nice as hers.
Sara:	Hey, who bought this photo album of cats in Rome?
David:	Jack, I think. Yes, it's his.
Jack:	What's mine?
David:	The photo album of cats in Rome.
Jack:	Oh, yes, that's ours.
Sara:	Ours?
Jack:	Mine and Emi's!
Emi:	Woof!

Comprehension

2 Answer the questions.

1 Did Sara like the holiday?
_____

2 Who did she buy a present for?
_____

3 Who bought the bigger Eiffel Tower?
_____

4 Does Mrs Doyle think Sara's present is nicer than David's?
_____

5 Where did Jack buy the photo album of cats?
_____

Vocabulary

3 Write an adjective and its opposite under the pictures.

> big   expensive   ~~tidy~~   old
> cheap   new   small   ~~untidy~~

bedroom

untidy   *tidy*

bicycle

1 _____ _____

mobile phone

2 _____ _____

CD collection

3 _____ _____

Communication

Look & Use

Yours is smaller than **mine**.
Whose is this?
It's **his**.
That's **ours**.

4 Work in pairs. Who do you think these objects belong to? Use *his*, *hers* or *theirs* in your sentences.

A *I think the tennis racket is Sally's.*
B *Yes, I agree. It's hers. / No, I think it's David's.*

Sounds Good!

5 Listen and repeat. Be careful of the 'h' sound!

His is heavier than hers, but hers is happier than ours.

Harry isn't very happy.

He's at home and he's ill but he's eating a ham sandwich.

My Turn

6 Work in groups of six. Collect one object from each person, and put them in a bag. Choose one, and tell the person beside you who it belongs to.

This is Francesco's. It's his.

7 In pairs, ask who each object belongs to. Answer first as a pair, then on your own.

A *Whose is this?*
B *It's ours. It's mine.*
 It's theirs. It's his / hers.

sixty-nine 69

8 Grammar Focus

Superlatives

Read the examples and complete the rules.

The Coliseum is one of **the oldest** monuments **in** the world.

Italians are **the craziest** drivers I know.

The most romantic place was the Trevi Fountain.

Oslo is **the most expensive** city **in** the world.

We use the _____ to compare one member of a group with the rest of the group.

We always use the definite article _____ before superlatives.

We use **of** or _____ after the superlative + noun.

Spelling

Read the examples and complete the rules.

Short adjectives			
old	**the** old**est**	high	**the** high**est**

For adjectives of **one syllable** we generally add **-est**.

thin	**the** thinn**est**	big	**the** bigg**est**

For adjectives of **one syllable** ending in consonant + one vowel + consonant we double the consonant and add _____.

late	**the** lat**est**	nice	**the** nic**est**

For adjectives of **one syllable** ending in _____ we add _____.

scary	**the** scar**iest**	crazy	**the** craz**iest**

For adjectives of **two syllables** ending in consonant + **y** we drop the _____ and add **-iest**.

Look at the examples and complete the rules.

Long adjectives	
expensive	**the most** expensive
romantic	**the most** romantic

For all other adjectives of two or more syllables we use _____ + adjective.

Irregular adjectives	
good	**the best**
bad	**the worst**
far	**the furthest**

Some superlative forms are irregular.

Think! We can use three patterns:

the + short adjective + **-est**

the _____ + long adjective

the + irregular _____

---

1 Write questions using superlative adjectives. Then write your answers.

what / difficult / subject / school?

A *What is the most difficult subject at school?*

B _____

1 where / beautiful / place / you know?

A _____

B _____

2 which / busy / time / of the day / for you?

A _____

B _____

3 what / good / TV programme?

A _____

B _____

4 what / nice / thing / you have got?

A _____

B _____

8

PT Grammar
- - - -> Superlatives p. 26
- - - -> Possessive pronouns p. 37

2 Use superlative adjectives to complete the leaflet for the airline. Then listen and check.

Basic Air is (cheap) _the cheapest_, (fast) _____, (safe) _____, and (efficient) _____ way for you to get from A to B.
Our seats are (big) _____ available for your comfort and the in-flight services are of (high) _____ quality.
Our staff are specially trained to provide you with (friendly) _____ service during your flight. Basic Air isn't basic – It's (good) _____!

Possessive pronouns

Read the examples and complete the rules.

Whose photo album is this?
Whose is this photo album?
The photo album of cats in Rome is **ours**.
Yours is smaller than **mine**.
Yours is just as nice as **hers**.
Whose football is this? It's **theirs**.

We use the question word _____ to ask for information about possession.
How do you say *whose* in your language?

The words in bold are possessive _____.

Look at the examples again and complete the table.

Possessive adjectives	Possessive pronouns
It's my album.	It's _mine_.
It's your album.	It's _____.
It's his album.	It's _____.
It's her album.	It's _____.
They're our albums.	They're _____.
They're your albums.	They're _____.
They're their albums.	They're _____.

Choose the correct options and get the rules.

There is / There isn't a noun after a possessive pronoun.

We *have / don't have* a possessive pronoun for things and animals.

We never use articles before possessive pronouns.

3 Complete the sentences. Write possessive pronouns for the underlined words.

This is my book.
It's _mine_.
1 This is your room.
   It's _____.
2 It isn't his MP3 player.
   It isn't _____.
3 Is it her guidebook?
   Is it _____?
4 These aren't our things!
   These aren't _____!
5 Are those your things?
   Are those _____?
6 These are all their things.
   These are all _____!

Electricity and Lightning

Electricity

1 Put the words in the right order to answer the question below.

What is electricity?

The _movement_ ___ ___ ___ ___ ___ ___ ___ ___. This is electricity!

> of energy ~~movement~~ produces of form a electrons

2 Listen and read the following text and tick (✓) T (True) or F (False).

Everything is made of atoms, they are very small particles. The centre of an atom is the nucleus. It contains protons and neutrons. Electrons orbit around the nucleus. Protons and electrons have an electrical charge. Protons have a 'positive' charge, electrons have a 'negative' charge. Neutrons have no charge. Electricity happens when electrons leave an atom.

	T	F
An atom is a large particle.	☐	✓
1 The nucleus is the centre of an atom.	☐	☐
2 A nucleus contains protons, neutrons and electrons.	☐	☐
3 Protons have a negative charge.	☐	☐
4 Electrons have a negative charge.	☐	☐
5 Neutrons have a negative charge.	☐	☐
6 Electricity happens when electrons reach the atom.	☐	☐

Who discovered electricity?

3 Match up the sentences to find out what Benjamin Franklin and Thomas Alva Edison in history are remembered for.

1. [C] Benjamin Franklin believed
2. [ ] Benjamin Franklin's kite experiment
3. [ ] Thomas Alva Edison invented
4. [ ] Thomas Alva Edison's most famous

A 1,093 things in the 1800s.
B proved electricity and lightning were the same thing.
C lightning was a natural form of electricity.
D invention is the light bulb.

Benjamin Franklin

Thomas Alva Edison

Project Time

Find out more about Ben Franklin's kite experiment and write a short report.

72 seventy-two

Staying Safe in a Lightning Storm

Electricity and Lightning

1 Match the pictures to the sentences to answer the question below. The pictures are in the correct order. Then listen and check.

1  2

3

What is lightning?

A ☐ Positively charged atoms go to the top of the cloud and negative atoms to the bottom.

B ☐ When the negatively charged atoms are at the bottom of the cloud and become crowded, they 'jump' to another part of the cloud, to a different cloud or to the ground. This 'jump' is electricity and is called lightning.

C ☐ Electrical charges develop inside a storm cloud.

During a lightning storm…

2 Match the pictures to the sentences and check with your teacher. Then draw the completed table in your notebook.

A Fly kites or model planes.
B Stay in the car or under a group of trees.
C Find shelter in a house or a small shed.
D Ride a bicycle.
E Drop anything you're carrying that's made of metal.
F Stay near windows and metal objects, such as radiators.
G Use a phone, unless it's an emergency.
H Stay low to the ground.
I Stand under an isolated tree or don't be the tallest thing around.
J Get away from water, wire fences, washing lines and metal pipes.

Project Time

Create a warning leaflet *'Safety in a Storm'*.
Use information from this page and your own ideas.

9 She was sitting next to you

1 Listen and read.

You were holding her!

Mrs Doyle: I can't help thinking we left something behind in Barcelona.
Sara: Our hearts maybe?
David: What do you think we forgot Mrs Doyle?
Mrs Doyle: Oh, I don't know. It's just a feeling!
David: Well, we've got the passports, the suitcases, the souvenirs, the dog...
ALL: The DOG!!!
Jack: S-T-O-P! Stop the van! Where's Emi?
David: She was sitting next to you in the van, wasn't she?
Jack: No, she wasn't! Sara was holding her on the lead when I last saw her.
Sara: No, I wasn't. She was behind the rubbish bins looking for food when I last saw her.
David: I'm sure she was in the van.
Jack: Turn the van around! EMI! EMI!
Sara: She wasn't on her lead. I'm sure she was eating behind the bins.
Mrs Doyle: Be quiet all of you. We're going straight back to Barcelona to find Emi and I think I know where she is!

Comprehension

2 Read the sentences and tick (✓) T (True) or F (False). Correct the false ones.

	T	F
Mrs Doyle thinks they left something in Barcelona.	✓	
1 They left their passports in Barcelona.		
2 They didn't leave their suitcases behind.		
3 David thought Emi was in the van.		
4 Sara saw Emi behind the bins.		
5 Mrs Doyle decides to continue their trip home.		

9

Vocabulary

3 Inside the camper van. Match the words to the pictures. Then listen and check. *C 2.18*

cooker ☐ door ☐ fridge ☐ mirror [1]
seat ☐ sink ☐ sofa-bed ☐
table ☐ toilet ☐ wardrobe ☐

4 Match the prepositions to the pictures. Then listen and check. *C 2.19*

behind   between   in   near   in front of
next to   ~~on~~   opposite   under

on

 1 _____
 2 _____

 3 _____
 4 _____
 5 _____

 6 _____
 7 _____
8 _____

Communication

Look & Use

She was sitting **next to** you.
She was eating **behind** the bins.

5 Work in pairs. Ask and answer questions about things inside the camper van.

passport?
A *Where is the passport?*
B *It's on the seat.*

1 suitcase?   3 table?
2 fridge?   4 sunglasses?

My Turn

6 Work in pairs. Student A: place some objects in different positions. Student B: turn your back and try to remember the position of each object.

A *There's a pen under the book.*
B *Yes, that's right. / No, it isn't under the book, it's...*

seventy-five **75**

9

1 Listen and read.

A little dog was looking for food

Jack: Emi! Emi!
Excuse me, I'm looking for my dog. She's white.

Person 1: Oh, yes! I saw a little white dog running into Park Güell.

Jack: Really? OK, thank you. Come on Mrs Doyle! Let's go into the park!

Mrs Doyle: Hello. Did you see a little white dog running into the park?

Person 2: No, but I saw a little dog near the bins. It was looking for food.

Jack: Quick Mrs Doyle! To the bins!

Person 3: Are you looking for your dog? A little dog was sleeping under the bench over there.

Mrs Doyle: *Moltes gràcies*.

Person 3: You're welcome!

Jack: Come on Mrs Doyle. Let's go over to the bench! Oh no! She's not here! Did you see a white dog near the bins?

Person 4: Yes. Five minutes ago two people were leaving the park with a little white dog...

Jack: Emi! Emi! Come back!

Comprehension

2 Match the beginnings and the ends of the sentences. Then put them in the correct order.

> near the bins   under a bench
> with two people   ~~into Park Güell~~

- [ ] **A** Finally she left the park _____.
- [1] **B** First she ran *into Park Güell* .
- [ ] **C** Next she looked for food _____.
- [ ] **D** Then she went to sleep _____.

Vocabulary

3 Match the words to the pictures. Then listen and check.

> bandstand ☐   bench ☐   bin ☐
> boating area ☐   flower bed ☐
> steps ☐   ice cream van ☐   lake [8]

76 seventy-six

Sounds Good!

 4 Listen to this magic spell. Then repeat it and invent one of your own.

> First count to three.
> Next climb a tree.
> Then find a key.
> Finally you're on holiday by the sea!

Communication

Look & Use

A dog **was sleeping** under the bench.
Two people **were leaving** the park.

5 Emi's rescuer tells her story. Put the events in the correct order to discover what happened to Emi.

Missing!
Last seen: Park Güell
Call 004479644365

- [ ] **A** My mum telephoned you.
- [ ] **B** When she saw you she was really happy.
- [ ] **C** We were having a picnic when we found Emi lying all alone under a park bench.
- [ ] **D** So we took her with us and we went home.
- [1] **E** When we were walking in the park we saw a missing poster with Emi's picture on it.
- [ ] **F** While we were waiting for you to arrive, Emi played in the garden.

 6 Compare your answers with your partner. Then listen and check.

7 Work in pairs. Prepare a telephone conversation between Jack and Isabel, Emi's rescuer.

Isabel: Say hello and introduce yourself. → **Jack:** Say hello and introduce yourself.

Isabel: Say that you found Emi in Park Güell. → **Jack:** Say that you lost her when you were leaving.

Isabel: Say that you were walking in the park when you saw Emi. → **Jack:** Say that you are very happy and thank her.

Isabel: Reply and ask where you can meet. → **Jack:** Say when and where you can meet.

Isabel: Say that it's OK and say goodbye. → **Jack:** Say goodbye.

8 Work in pairs. Design your own park with the items from exercise 3. Then describe it to the class.

A *In our park there is a big lake on the left and a little fountain.*

B *Yes, and near the lake there are five ice cream vans open 24 hours a day!*

My Turn

9 Work in pairs. Ask and answer the following questions, then invent one of your own.

1. What were you doing at eight o'clock last night?
2. Where were you living when you were six months old?
3. Who were you talking to before this English lesson began?
4. What were you thinking about a minute ago?
5. _____?

9 Grammar Focus

Past continuous

Affirmative form

Look at the examples. How do you say these sentences in your language?

*She **was sitting** next to you.*
*She **was sleeping** under the bench.*
*Two people **were leaving** the park.*
*They **were looking** for Emi.*

We use the past continuous (also called: progressive) to describe an action in progress in the past.

Read the examples again and complete the sentence pattern.

We make the affirmative form of the past continuous with:

subject + *was* / _____ + _____ form of the main verb.

Negative form

Read the examples and complete the pattern.

*I **wasn't sleeping**.*
*He **wasn't wearing** jeans.*
*We **weren't listening** to the teacher.*
*You **weren't looking** at the road map.*

In the negative form the sentence pattern is:

subject + _____ / _____ + *-ing* form of the main verb.

1 What was happening in your house at 9 p.m. last night? Write four positive sentences using the past continuous.

> *I was studying English.*
> *Dad was cooking.*
> *My brother and sister were...*
> *On TV a man was...*

2 Use the expressions to describe what the people were doing.

~~jogging~~   reading a newspaper
riding a bike   sunbathing

When Mrs Doyle and Jack arrived at the park...

two people were jogging.

1 _____

2 _____

3 _____

Questions and short answers

Look at the examples and complete the patterns.

*What **were you** doing?*
*Where **was she** going?*
*Why **were they** crying?*

***Were you** studying? No, **I wasn't**.*
***Were they** smiling? Yes, **they were**.*
***Was I** dreaming? Yes, **you were**!*

In questions the sentence pattern is:

_____ / _____ + subject + _____ form of the main verb.

In short answers the sentence pattern is:

Yes, + subject + _____ / _____.
No, + _____ + _____ / _____.

Wh- words (*What, Where, Why...*) generally go before the verb *be*.

PT Grammar
----> Past continuous pp. 71-74
----> Linkers (2) p. 75

9

3 Write questions for these answers.

What were you doing in London last week?
I was shopping with my mum.

1 What _____?
We were watching television at 9 p.m.
2 Why _____?
They were running to catch the bus.
3 Was _____?
No, he wasn't. He was playing football.
4 Was _____?
No, she wasn't. She was showing me pictures of her holiday.

Past simple vs Past continuous

when

Read the example, look at the pattern, and choose the correct option.

We were walking in the park when we found a little lost dog.

... **when** we found ...

We were walking ...

We use the *past simple / past continuous* to describe an action in progress at a specified time in the past.

We often use the *past simple / past continuous* to say that something happened during an action in progress in the past.

We can link the past simple and the past continuous with **when**.
*You were holding her on the lead **when** I last saw her.*

We use **when** + past simple if we want to say that an action happened after another.
*I went to bed **when** I finished my homework.*

C 2.24

4 Complete the sentences with the past simple or the past continuous of the verbs in brackets. Then listen and check.

I _was going_ to bed when the phone _rang_ . (go / ring)
1 While they _____ on the beach, it _____ to rain. (sit / start)
2 You _____ when I _____ at the party. (leave / arrive)
3 He _____ the road when the car _____ suddenly. (cross / stop)
4 They _____ in class when the headmaster _____ in. (sit / come)

Linkers (2)

Sequencing adverbs

Write the sequencing adverbs in order.

first   finally   then / next

1 _____
2 _____
3 _____

Read the examples. How do you say these adverbs in your language?

First Emi ran into Park Güell.
Then / Next she looked for food.
Finally she left the park.

Circle the correct option and get the rule.

When we want to describe a sequence of actions we use sequencing adverbs + *past simple / past continuous*.

seventy-nine **79**

9 CURIOSITY CORNER

1 Did you know?

Do you find Maths or English difficult? Take a look at the length of your fingers. Experts believe there is a link between kids' ability in Maths and English tests and the lengths of their index and ring fingers. If your ring finger is longer than your index finger you are better at Maths. If it's shorter, English is the subject for you!

2 Joke Time

Why did the tomato blush?

Because it saw the salad dressing.

3 Incredible!

It takes the average snail eight and a half hours to travel the length of the football pitch in Wembley Stadium, London!

4 Riddle Time

What letter comes once in a year, twice in a week and never in a day?

The letter E.

5 Fun Fact

According to the Guinness Book of Records, the tallest man in the world is Leonid Stadnyk. He comes from the Ukraine and is 8ft 5ins (2.57 metres) tall.

ft (foot): 30.48 cm
in (inch): 2.54 cm

CURIOSITY CORNER 9

6 Wordsearch

Look at the pictures.
Find these animals in the puzzle.
Then use the remaining letters
to find the hidden saying.

K _I_ _T_ _T_ _E_ N

```
L I O N M A N
P E A C O C K
B E S T U F R
F O X I S E N
D H I S E D O
G K I T T E N
```

1 F _ X

3 L _ _ _ N

2 P _ _ _ _ _ _ K

4 M _ _ _ _ E

A M _ _ 'S _ _ _ _ _ _
_ _ _ _ _ _ _ IS _ _ _ _
_ _ _ !

7 Animal Crazy!

The British people love their pets. In fact, they are a nation of 'animal lovers' who regard their pets as a member of the family.

Once a year there is National Pet Month when people celebrate their animal friends!

What is the most popular pet in the UK?
- [ ] A cat
- [ ] B dog
- [ ] C rabbit

8 As slow as a snail!

C 2.25 In English we often compare people and things to animals. Complete the following phrases with one of the animals from the wordsearch. Then listen and check.

As playful as a *kitten.*
1 As brave as a _____
2 As quiet as a _____
3 As sly as a _____
4 As proud as a _____

9 Animal Quiz – True or False?

	T	F
1 Most animals are colour-blind.	☐	☐
2 There are no snakes in Ireland.	☐	☐
3 Birds have no teeth.	☐	☐
4 Hummingbirds can fly backwards.	☐	☐
5 Only female mosquitoes bite humans.	☐	☐
6 Dogs and cats dream when they sleep.	☐	☐

Units 7-9 Check Your Progress

1 Complete the diagram with adjectives.

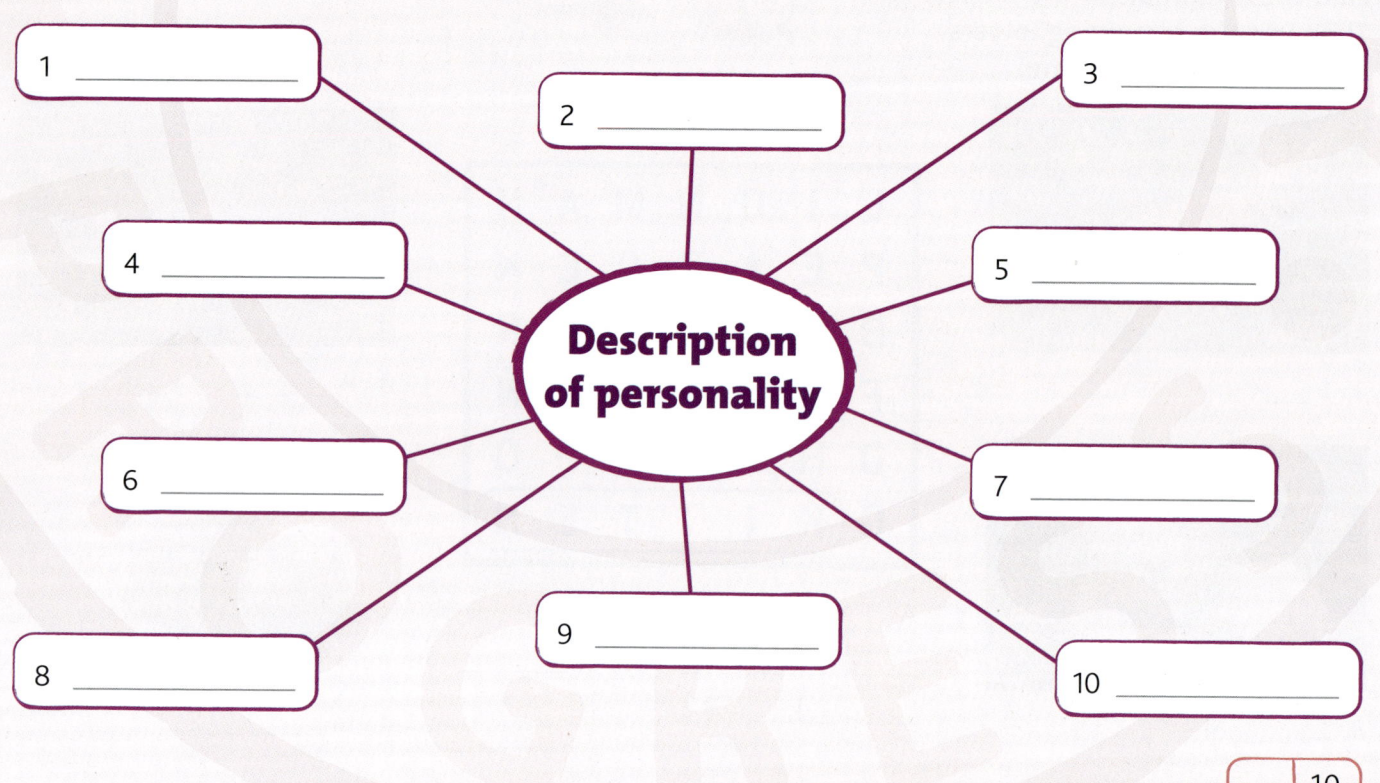

1 _____
2 _____
3 _____
4 _____
5 _____
6 _____
7 _____
8 _____
9 _____
10 _____

Description of personality

☐ / 10

2 Write the opposites of the adjectives.
1 clean _____
2 boring _____
3 expensive _____
4 long _____
5 noisy _____

☐ / 5

3 Look at the picture and correct the sentences.
1 There's a book behind the cooker.
_____
2 The glass is next to the sofa.
_____
3 The dog is under the table.
_____
4 The flowers are in the sink.
_____

☐ / 8

82   eighty-two

Units 7-9

4 Look at the photos and complete the sentences using the comparative or superlative form of the adjectives in brackets.

1 The motorbike is the _____ (expensive).
2 The bicycle is _____ (cheap) than the moped.
3 The motorbike is _____ (fast) than the moped.
4 The bicycle is the _____ (cheap).
5 The moped is _____ (slow) than the motorbike.

☐ 5

5 Write complete sentences using the superlative form of each adjective. Remember to use the article!

(beautiful) actress in the world
Julia Roberts is the most beautiful actress in the world.

1 (good) actor in the world
   _____
2 (boring) film ever
   _____
3 (bad) singer in the world
   _____
4 (exciting) sport
   _____
5 (interesting) place in my country
   _____

☐ 5

6 Circle the correct word to complete the sentences.

1 That bike is *your / mine*!
2 This is my sister's bedroom, but this laptop isn't *hers / his*.
3 Which coat is *you / yours*?
4 This is Michael's dog. But whose is this tortoise? Is it *him / his* too?
5 A Is this *ours / our*?
   B No dear, it's Lucy's.

☐ 5

7 Complete the police report with the past simple or past continuous of the verbs in brackets.

POLICE DEPARTMENT
****

Friday, 16th September – 6.30 p.m.
William Smith

I (1) _____ (walk) home from school this afternoon when I (2) _____ (see) three men get out of a car and run towards the bank in Lowhill Road. They (3) _____ (wear) black trousers, blue jackets and balaclavas.
I (4) _____ (stop) and (5) _____ (watch) them. Suddenly another man (6) _____ (get) out of the car. He (7) _____ (talk) to someone on his mobile phone. He (8) _____ (be) about 50 and he (9) _____ (wear) a blue jacket and red trousers. He (10) _____ (not wear) a balaclava, so I (11) _____ (take) a picture of him with my mobile phone and I (12) _____ (send) it to the police!

☐ 12

My final score is: ☐ 50

10 We could join a club

1 Listen and read.

You can't go down that street!

David: Look! We're only 15 kilometres from Nantes.
Jack: Can we go into the city? I wanted to go to Lyon, but you said there wasn't time.
David: OK, OK! Let's hope it's as nice as Paris!

Later
David: Let's see. Which way?
Mrs Doyle: David, there's a *No entry* sign. You can't go down that street.
David: Oops, yes, you're right. Oh, and I can't turn left there.
Jack: But you can turn right here. Look, there's a sign for the city centre.
Mrs Doyle: David, be careful! There's no overtaking here!
David: Sorry...
Sara: David, stop! We can't drive into the city centre today – it's Sunday!!
David: What?!
Mrs Doyle: Why don't we find a place to park?
David: Not here... look at all those *No Parking* signs.
Sara: Don't worry – it says in the guidebook that you can leave the camper van at the *Park 'n' Ride*. Then you can get the bus to the city centre. It only costs 2 euros each.
David: Good idea! I'm sure a parking fine is more expensive than that!

Comprehension

2 Answer the questions.
1. Where are they?
2. Why didn't they go to Lyon?
3. What day is it?
4. Can they drive into the city centre?
5. Can they leave the camper van in the *Park 'n' Ride*?
6. How can they get to the city centre?

Vocabulary

3 Match the words to the road signs.

A No overtaking   E No parking
B No right turn   F No left turn
C One-way   G Give right of way
D Parking   H No entry

B 1

2 3

4 5

6 7

 4 Listen and check.

Communication

Look & Use

Can we go into the city?
We can get the bus.
We can't drive into the city centre.

6 Listen to Alex and Sharon. Then tick (✓) the correct box to complete the sentences.

	can	can't	
Sharon	☐	✓	do her homework after dinner.
1 Alex	☐	☐	call Sharon at six o'clock.
2 Sharon	☐	☐	stay on the phone for more than ten minutes.
3 Sharon	☐	☐	surf the Internet for one hour a day.
4 Sharon	☐	☐	listen to loud music.
5 Alex	☐	☐	watch TV until 11 p.m.

7 Check your answers with your partner.

A *Can Sharon do her homework after dinner?*
B *No, she can't.*

My Turn

8 What can you do at home? Write sentences using *can* or *can't*.

> stay up until 10 p.m.
> surf the Internet for more than one hour a day
> listen to loud music in my bedroom
> watch television until 10.30 p.m.
> stay on the phone for more than half an hour
> do my homework after dinner
> see my friends during the week
> stay out until 11 p.m. on Saturday nights

I can watch television until 10.30 p.m.

9 Work in pairs. Ask your partner questions to find out what he / she can or can't do at home.

A *Can you stay up until ten o'clock?*
B *Yes, I can. / No, I can't.*

eighty-five **85**

10

 1 Listen and read.

Could you teach me how to play?

Jack: Hey Sara, could you pass me the camera, please? I want to take the last few photos.
Sara: Here you are. Ah, we're nearly home! I can't imagine the Camp without all our friends.
David: Yeah, the Camp is boring when there are no guests.
Mrs Doyle: Well, why don't you take up a hobby, join a club…
David: Well, I can play chess.
Sara: Could you teach me how to play?
Jack: That sounds boring! Could we join a kick-boxing club?
Mrs Doyle: … I don't know about that. It sounds a bit violent.
David: I know how to keep busy! Mrs Doyle, could we organise a party at the Camp? We could invite Maria and Natalie and everyone we know!
Mrs Doyle: That's a great idea! You can all help.

Comprehension

2 Read the following sentences and tick (✓) T (True) or F (False). Then correct the false ones.

	T	F
Jack has got the camera.	☐	✓
Sara has got the camera.		
1 Sara doesn't know how to play chess.	☐	☐
2 Jack wants to learn to play chess too.	☐	☐
3 Mrs Doyle likes Jack's idea.	☐	☐
4 Mrs Doyle likes David's idea.	☐	☐

Vocabulary

 3 Match the activities to the pictures. Then listen and check.

> play chess   ~~go hiking~~   learn a language
> do kick-boxing   go horse riding

go hiking

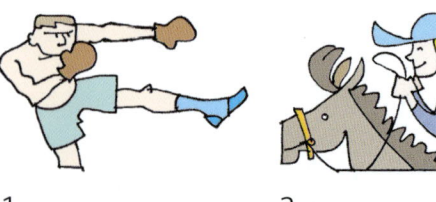

1 _____   2 _____

3 _____   4 _____

86 eighty-six

10

 4 Complete the requests with the following verbs. Then listen and check.

> lend ~~borrow~~ play teach speak

Could I _borrow_ your notebook, please?
1 Can I _____ chess with you?
2 Can I _____ my language in my English class?
3 Could you _____ me your dictionary, please?
4 Could you _____ me kick-boxing?

Hot Tip!

Don't confuse *borrow* and *lend*!
Borrow is when **someone gives you something**. **Lend** is when **you give something to someone**.

*Could **I** borrow your pen, please?*
*Could **you** lend me your pen, please?*

Sounds Good!

 5 Listen to the rhyme. Then repeat it.

> There was a lady called May
> She said borrow comes towards you
> And lend goes away
> Say please and thank you
> And you'll have a great day!

Communication

Look & Use

Could we organise a party at the Camp?
We **could** invite Maria and Natalie.

6 Work in pairs. Ask and answer questions.

chess set, riding hat, boots, boxing gloves, dictionary

You want to play chess.
A *Could I borrow your chess set, please?*
B *Yes, you can. / No, sorry. I need it.*
or
A *Could you lend me your chess set, please?*
B *Yes, of course. / No, sorry. I need it.*
1 You have a kick-boxing lesson.
2 You have a Spanish test.
3 You have a horse riding lesson.
4 You want to go hiking.

My Turn

7 You want to borrow three things from your teacher. Ask him / her.

A *Could I borrow your ruler, please?*
B *Yes, of course.*
A *Could you lend me your History book, please?*
B *No, sorry. I need it.*

10 Grammar Focus

can – ability

Read the examples. How do you say *can* and *can't* in your language?

Can you play the violin?

No, I *can't*. But I *can* play the drums.

Complete the rule.

We use the verb _____ / _____ to say that a person has, or doesn't have the **ability** to do things in the present.

can – permission

Read the examples then complete the explanations. How do you say *can* and *can't* in your language?

You **can't** turn left here.

But you **can** turn right here.

When we talk about rules, we use _____ / _____ to say that something is (**permission**), or isn't (**prohibition**) allowed.

Can I go out, Mum?

No, you **can't**.

We use *Can...?* to ask for _____ .
We use _____ to refuse permission.
To give permission we say:
Yes, you _____ .

1 Complete the dialogues using *can* or *can't*.

1. A Mum, _can_ I go to Emma's party?
   B Yes, you _____ .
   A _____ I come home at midnight?
   B No, you _____ !
2. A _____ we go to the cinema tomorrow night?
   B No, you _____ , but you _____ do your homework!
3. A _____ I have chips for lunch?
   B No, you _____ .
   A What _____ I have?
   B You _____ have carrots. They're good for you!

2 What rules are there in a library? Complete the notice with *can* or *can't*.

Public Library

You _can_ borrow three books per day.
You (1) _____ speak on your mobile phone.
You (2) _____ eat in the library.
You (3) _____ buy food in the café.
You (4) _____ read books in the reading room.

can / could – requests

Read the examples and complete the patterns.

Can you close the window, please? I'm cold!

Could you teach me how to play?

We can make **requests** (ask people to do something) with:

_____ + subject + base form + ... ?

We can make more formal and **polite requests** with:

_____ + subject + base form + ... ?

10

PT Grammar
- Modal verbs: can / could pp. 100-101, 109
- lend / borrow p.137

3 Reorder the requests.

you / please / repeat / that / could / ?
Could you repeat that, please?

1 the / open / me / for / can / door / you / please / ?
2 pass / could / me / please / you / salt / the / ?
3 your / tell / name / you / could / me / please / ?
4 my / with / can / homework / help / please / me / you / ?

could – possibility

Read the examples. How do you say *could* in your language?

David **could** teach us how to play chess.

I **couldn't** concentrate long enough to play chess!

Could we join a kick-boxing club?

Complete the rules.

We use _____ + base form to talk about **possible** or impossible actions in the present.

In the negative form the pattern is:
subject + _____ + base form

In questions the pattern is:
_____ + subject + _____ _____ + ... ?

C 2.33

4 Complete the sentences with *could* or *couldn't* and one of the following verbs. Then listen and check.

eat   go   help   live   run

1 _____ you _____ me with the washing up?
2 I _____ in Iceland. It's too cold!
3 Simon runs every morning. He _____ _____ a marathon.
4 We _____ for a walk on Sunday.
5 I'm so hungry. I _____ a horse!

could – short answers

Read the examples and complete the pattern.

Could we have a disco?
Yes, we **could**!
No, we **couldn't**. The neighbours don't like loud music.

Could your mother cook dinner for 100 people?
Yes, she **could**!
No, she **couldn't**. She hasn't got enough pots and pans.

In **short answers** the pattern is:
Yes, + subject + *could*.

No, + _____ + _____.

5 Write the questions and complete the short answers.

1 you / walk 10 miles?
_____? Yes, _____!
2 your best friend / count to 1,000 in English?
_____? No, _____!
3 your uncle / beat your neighbour at tennis?
_____? Yes, _____!
4 your partner / eat three pizzas for dinner?
_____? No, _____!

10

Reading

1 Read the information about Disney World and answer the questions.

1 What can you do in *Hollywood Boulevard*?
2 Where can you learn about international culture and technological innovation?
3 What can you experience on the *Motion Simulator*?
4 Where can you learn about animal conservation?
5 What can you see in the *Tree of Life*?

Enjoy Disney World!

Discover all the fun things there are to do!

Disney's Hollywood Studios

At this park the theme is TV and movies. *Hollywood Boulevard* is the ideal place to buy food and souvenirs or you can watch the spectacular *Disney Stars and Motor Cars Parade*. On the *Backlot Tour* there are incredible stunts to see, plus you can learn all about special effects. At *Animation Courtyard* there are live shows featuring puppets, actors and incredible lasers.

Epcot

The *Epcot* theme park is dedicated to international culture and technological innovation. There is a 13-minute *Dark Ride* where you can explore the progression of human communications from cavemen to the birth of the Internet.
Or how about the *Motion Simulator* where you can experience space travel – just like a real astronaut!

Disney's Animal Kingdom

This is the largest Disney theme park in the world and it's all about animal conservation. Wear walking shoes and prepare to explore a kingdom of animals. The *African Safari* is a truly amazing experience.
So what else is there to do here? Well, you can meet Mickey and Minnie Mouse of course, and at the spectacular *Rainforest Café* there's great food for all the family. Plus, don't forget to stop at the *Tree of Life* where you can watch a 3-D film all about bugs.

Can you resist coming to Disney World?

10

Speaking

2 Work in pairs. Ask and answer questions to decide what you can do and where.

Student A	Student B
These are the things you want to do in Disney World: - go on safari - see a live show - travel back in time	These are the things you want to do in Disney World: - learn about special effects - meet famous Disney characters - experience space travel

A *What do you want to do in Disney World?*

B *I really want to meet some famous Disney characters.*

A *OK. We can go to the Animal Kingdom and meet Mickey Mouse.*

B *Great! What about you? What do you want to do?*

A *I want to see a live show.*

B *You can do that at the Hollywood studios.*

Listening

3 Listen to the information about Loch Ness in Scotland and use the words to fill in the gaps.

could   have   largest
biggest   deepest

Come to Loch Ness in the Scottish Highlands and you could (1) _____ a very unusual experience.
'Loch' means 'lake' in Gaelic. Loch Ness is the second (2) _____ Scottish loch after Loch Lomond, but, because its (3) _____ point is 230 m, it is considered the (4) _____.
Loch Ness is famous for the mysterious Loch Ness Monster, also know as 'Nessie'.
So, come to Loch Ness.
You (5) _____ meet 'Nessie'!

Writing

4 Now write your own holiday leaflet for a desert island. Draw a picture and describe the island (where it is and what it's like). Say what you can and can't do there.

11 Everybody likes parties

1 Listen and read.

Has anybody got any ideas?

David: OK. So who wants to buy food and drink for the party on Saturday?
Sara: Me! I love shopping!
Mrs Doyle: Me too. We can buy everything at the new supermarket in town.
Sara: What about music? Has anybody got any ideas?
David: I know somebody who's a DJ, so I can organise the music.
Sara: Great!
David: Does anybody like making invitations?
Jack: Boring! Nobody likes doing that.
Sara: Oh, I like making things.
Jack: What can I do?
Sara: You can decorate the TV room with balloons and streamers.
Jack: Brilliant! I love decorating things!
David: OK. Is that everything?
Sara: No, I've got an idea. Why don't we make it a fancy dress party?
David: Fancy dress?
Sara: Yes, we can tell everyone to make costumes.
David: I think I've got an old *Superman* costume somewhere.

Comprehension

2 Complete David's notes about the party.

Things to do for the party on _Saturday_.

- Sara and (1) _____ can buy (2) _____ and (3) _____ at the supermarket.
- I (David) can organise the (4) _____. (5) _____ can make (6) _____.
- Jack can (7) _____ the TV room with (8) _____ and streamers.
- Remember to tell everyone to make (9) _____ for a fancy dress party!

92   ninety-two

11

Vocabulary

Pyjama party
~~Birthday party~~
Fancy Dress party
Halloween party
New Year's Eve party

 3 Match the types of party to the pictures. Then listen and check.

Birthday party   1 _____   2 _____

3 _____   4 _____

Communication

Look & Use

I **like** mak**ing** invitations.
I **love** decorat**ing** things!

4 Work in pairs. What type of party do you like and why? Ask and answer questions. Use the words in the box to help you.

> make invitations   ~~sleep in sleeping bags~~
> eat party food   organise music
> make costumes   sleep at a friend's house
> buy food and drink   decorate rooms
> receive / give presents

A *Do you like Pyjama parties?*
B *Yes. I like sleeping in sleeping bags.*

My Turn

5 Work in groups. You are organising a party. First make a list of things to do. Then ask your classmates who's doing what and take notes.

> *A Fancy Dress party*
> *- make costumes (Ted)*
> *- buy food and drink (Jane)*

A *Does anybody like making costumes?*
B *I love making costumes.*

6 Report the information back to the class.

Ted likes making costumes. Jane likes...

11

1 Listen and read.

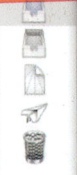

Everyone got dressed up!

Dear Sophie,

Hi! How are you?
We had a fantastic party last weekend! It was a fancy dress party and everyone got dressed up. I was Catwoman and David came in a Superman costume! He looked really funny!
Nobody knew where Jack was at the beginning of the party – when he arrived he was wearing a big white sheet over his head and he said he was a ghost! Everybody laughed!

We had a great time! I was dancing with Natalie and David was chatting to a girl – I think he liked her! And Jack was telling Maria jokes, but she didn't get his jokes. Poor Maria! Jack's jokes are terrible!

I nearly forgot! Mrs Doyle came as Queen Elizabeth I. She didn't tell anybody about her costume, so it was a big surprise for everyone. Oh, and Emi was there too. She had a great time – she was barking loudly and running around all the time.

Write soon,
Bye!
Sara

Comprehension

2 Read Sara's e-mail again and complete the sentences.

David was wearing *a Superman costume*.

1 Sara was dancing with…
2 Jack was…
3 Mrs Doyle got dressed up as…
4 Emi had…

Vocabulary

3 Match the expressions to the pictures. Then listen and check.

get married

1 _____

2 _____

get old   get tired
~~get married~~
get dressed up
get lost

3 _____

4 _____

94 ninety-four

11

 4 Complete the sentences with a word from the box. Then listen and check.

> nobody   everybody   somebody   anybody

1 Did _____ call me?
2 _____ broke the window.

3 There's _____ at home.
4 _____ sang 'Happy Birthday!'

Sounds Good!

 5 Listen and repeat.

There's someone at the door.

 6 Listen and repeat the following sentences. Then mark the stress on the words 'anyone', 'nobody' and 'everyone'.

Does anyone want to go to the cinema?
I'm sad. Nobody remembered my birthday!
Everyone was at the party.

Communication

Look & Use

Everyone got dressed up.
Nobody knew where Jack was.
She didn't tell **anybody** about her costume.
Does **anyone** want to go to the cinema?

7 Work in pairs. Student A: look at the picture below. Student B: look at the picture on page 121. Ask and answer questions.

A *Is anybody dancing in your picture?*
B *Yes, somebody is dancing.*
A *Is anybody drinking?*
B *No, nobody is drinking.*

 8 Work in pairs. Take turns to ask and answer questions. Then listen and check.

> ~~7 a.m.~~   In 1996.   Yes, I was a robot.
> Yes, he's 10 years old now!

you / get up / this morning?
 A *What time did you get up this morning?*
 B *At 7 a.m.*

1 your mum and dad / get married?
2 you / get dressed up / for the party?
3 your dog / get old?

My Turn

9 Answer these questions.

1 What time did you get up last Sunday?
2 Do you always get someone's jokes?
3 Are you going anywhere next weekend?
4 Did you do anything funny last weekend?
5 Is there anything you don't want to tell anybody?

ninety-five   **95**

11 Grammar Focus

someone, anything, everywhere, etc.

We use compounds with *some, any, no, every* to talk about indefinite people, things, places.

Read the examples and complete the tables.

We can buy **everything** at the new supermarket in town.

Has **anybody** got any ideas?

I know **somebody** who's a DJ.

I've got an old Superman costume **somewhere**.

	Affirmative	Affirmative
People	somebody / someone	everybody _____
Things	_____	everything
Places	somewhere	everywhere

	Negative	Negative / Questions
People	_____ / no one	anybody / anyone
Things	nothing	anything
Places	nowhere	_____

Read these examples. Then choose the correct option and get the rule.

Nobody likes making invitations.

There is **nothing** to do here. I'm bored!

With *nobody, nothing, nowhere* we use the **affirmative / negative** form of the verb.

1 Complete the words with *some, every, any* or *no*.

Is there __any__ thing in the fridge?

1 I really want to go _____where hot this summer.

2 All my friends came to my birthday party and _____body brought a present! I was really lucky!

3 I'm really bored. I've got _____thing to do this afternoon.

4 _____one stop writing now! The exam is finished.

5 I know _____one who lives in Spain.

2 Substitute the underlined words with *someone, anything, everywhere*, etc.

There's <u>a person</u> at the front door.
 someone

1 I haven't got <u>a thing</u> to wear to the party.
 _____

2 There is <u>no food</u> in the fridge.
 _____

3 There are bees <u>in every place</u>.
 _____

4 Is <u>a person</u> at home?
 _____

5 I did <u>all the things</u> I wanted to do.
 _____

11

> **PT Grammar**
> → *someone*, etc. p. 76
> → *get* + adj. / past part. p. 122
> → Verbs and adj. + *-ing* form p. 58

get

Match the examples to the meanings of the verb *get*.

1 *What time did you **get** to the party?*
2 *Did you **get** any e-mails today?*
3 *Can you **get** some bread at the supermarket?*
4 *I don't think she **gets** his jokes.*

☐ **A** get = buy
☐ **B** get = understand
☐ **C** get = arrive
☐ **D** get = receive

The verb *get* can have different meanings. In conversation we often use the verb *get* instead of other verbs.

Read these expressions with *get*. How do you say them in your language?

get lost	get cold
get tired	get old
get worried	get wet
get married	get ready

Look at the expressions again and complete the rule.

For some verbs that may be reflexive in other languages we can use *get* + past participle or we can use _____ + _____.

Get + adjective can mean *become*.

3 Substitute the underlined verbs with the correct forms of the verbs in the box.

> understand   arrive in   bought
> ~~earns~~   receive   become

My brother <u>gets</u> lots of money in his new job.
   earns

1 Is your cat <u>getting</u> older?
   _____

2 I didn't <u>get</u> that joke.
   _____

3 Did she <u>get</u> a lot of birthday cards?
   _____

4 I <u>got</u> a new dress today.
   _____

5 What time does the train <u>get to</u> London?
   _____

4 Rewrite the sentences using the appropriate expressions with *get*.

> She received 25 birthday cards this year!
> *She got 25 birthday cards this year!*

1 My grandmother is becoming older and older!
2 We bought lots of food and drink for the party.
3 She arrived home at 3 o'clock.
4 My brother and his girlfriend became husband and wife last August.

Verbs + -ing form

Read the examples and complete the rule.

*Does anybody **like making** invitations?*

*I **love decorating** things!*

After *like / love / hate*, etc. we use the _____ form of the main verb.

5 Complete the sentences with the *-ing* form of the verb in brackets.

> Sara loves ___*playing*___ (play) cards.

1 My sister doesn't like _____ (go) to the dentist.
2 We really like _____ (watch) football on TV.
3 I hate _____ (snowboard) in the winter.
4 My dad likes _____ (cycle) to work.
5 My cousin loves _____ (run) the London Marathon. He does it every year!

ninety-seven **97**

CLIL Earthquakes

What are earthquakes?

1 Look at the picture and fill in the gaps with the words below, then listen and check.

> million   earthquake   energy   plates   ~~continents~~

In the beginning all the continents in the world were joined together. This was called *Pangaea*. The ___continents___ slowly started to separate and continue to move today.

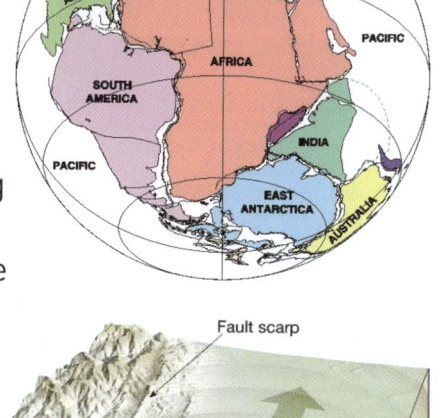

Earthquakes are sudden shocks, shaking or rolling of the earth's surface. There are more than a (1) _____ earthquakes in the world each year.

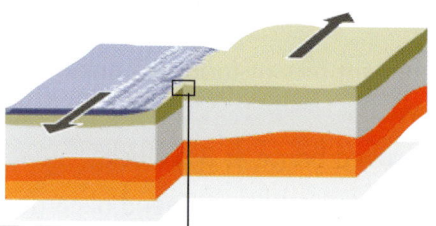

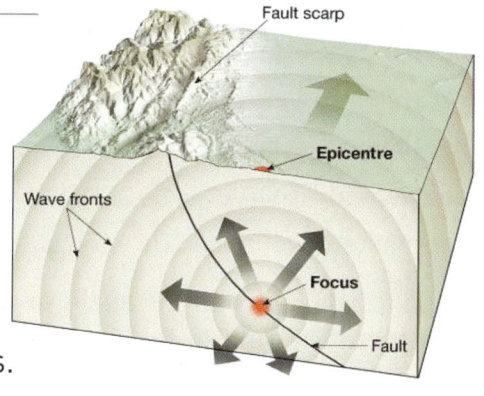

As the plates move they put forces on themselves and each other. When the force is great enough, the Earth's crust breaks. This stress is released as energy. The (2) _____ moves through the earth as waves.

There are about twenty (3) _____ along the surface of the earth. They move continuously and slowly past each other. When the plates squeeze or stretch, large rocks form at their edges. The rocks move causing an (4) _____ .

2 Work in pairs. Underline the key information about earthquakes in the text.

Project Time

Find out about the meaning of these words that relate to the topic earthquakes and report back to the class.

> epicentre   seismograph   Richter scale

98   ninety-eight

Earthquake Safety Tips

1. **What are the three key things to remember in an earthquake? Complete the sentences with the verbs in the box.**

   cover
   hold on
   drop

   1 _____ to the ground and stay under something strong.
   2 _____ and protect your head by pressing your face against your arm.
   3 _____ to something strong and be prepared to shake with it.

What to do *before* an earthquake.

2. **Match the items in your 'Disaster Supplies Kit' with the words below.**

   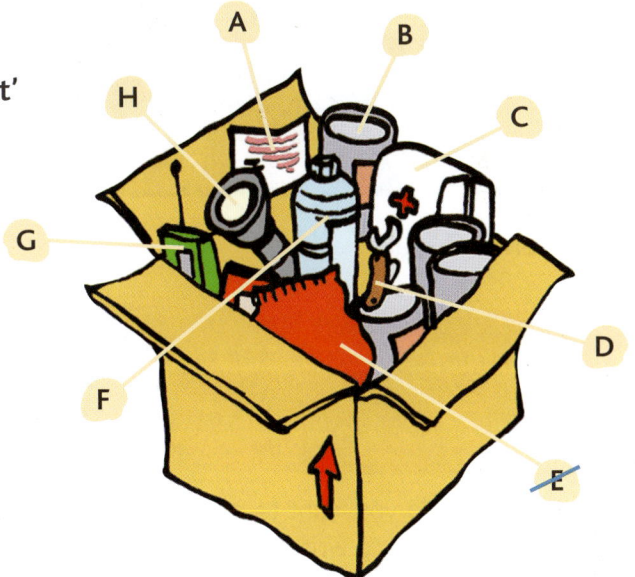

   - [E] protective clothing
   - 1 [ ] canned food
   - 2 [ ] battery-operated radio
   - 3 [ ] torch
   - 4 [ ] first aid kit
   - 5 [ ] bottled water
   - 6 [ ] written instructions on how to turn off electricity, gas and water
   - 7 [ ] can opener

3. **Play the Memory Game. Look at the Disaster Supplies Kit for thirty seconds and then close your books. See how many important items you can remember.**

What to do *during* an earthquake.

4. **Complete the sentences by matching up the two halves to learn what to do during an earthquake. Then listen and check.**

   1 [B] If you're outdoors,
   2 [ ] If you're in bed,
   3 [ ] If you're indoors,
   4 [ ] If you're in a car,

   A go under your bed.
   B find a clear spot away from buildings, trees and power lines. Then drop to the ground.
   C slow down and drive to a safe place.
   D stay away from windows.

Project Time

Draw a map of your home and mark safe places on it remembering the three key safety tips: drop, cover and hold on.

12 Are you coming back?

1 Listen and read.

I'm going to send José an e-mail

David: Hey Sara, do you want to come to the park?
Sara: No, I'm going to write José an e-mail in the Internet room.
David: Oh, you can't!
Sara: Why not?
David: The computers aren't working today.
Sara: But I need a computer.
David: Don't worry, you can use my new laptop.
Sara: Your laptop?
David: Yes, look! It's got a webcam and a big screen and…
Sara: OK! Thanks David.
David: So, are you going to tell José about the weather?
Sara: No, David, I'm *not* going to tell him about the weather.
I'm going to tell him about the party.
David: Right, well, remember to tell him that we're going to chat online to Paolo and Francesco on Friday.

Comprehension

2 Tick (✓) the correct answer.

Is Sara going to the park with David?
☐ **A** Yes, she is.   ✓ **B** No, she isn't.

1 Is she going to send José an e-mail?
☐ **A** Yes, she is.   ☐ **B** No, she isn't.

2 Whose is the laptop?
☐ **A** It's Sara's.   ☐ **B** It's David's.

3 Has the laptop got a webcam?
☐ **A** Yes, it has.   ☐ **B** No, it hasn't.

4 Are they going to meet Paolo on Friday?
☐ **A** Yes, they are.   ☐ **B** No, they aren't.

12

Vocabulary

3 Match the phrases to the pictures. Then listen and check.

meet my friends   buy some clothes
do some research on the Internet   call my friend
do a school project   train for the football match

meet my friends   1 _____   2 _____   3 _____   4 _____   5 _____

4 Reorder the jumbled words and match them to the objects in the picture. Then listen and check.

SEKESRAP — G speakers
1 RIPTNRE
2 DKYEOARB
3 RENSCE
4 NSRENAC
5 OMSEU
6 WETOR CP

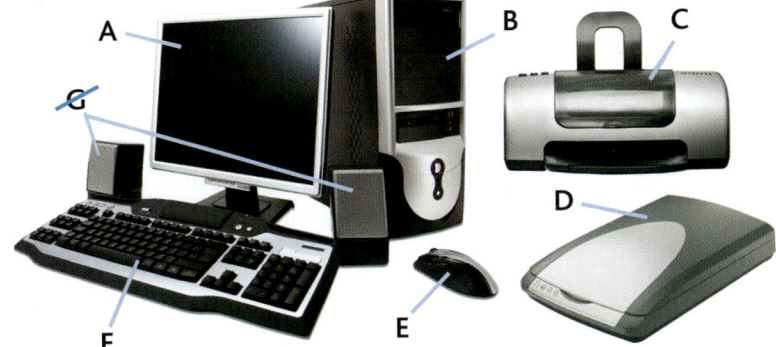

5 Now write a list of other computer words you know.

Communication

Look & Use

We**'re going to chat** online on Friday.
Are you **going to tell** José about the weather?

6 In pairs, ask and answer questions about what you are going to do on Saturday.

do your homework   meet your friends
buy some clothes   train for the football match
visit your grandparents   go to a party

A *Are you going to meet your friends on Saturday?*
B *Yes, I am. / No, I'm not.*

Sounds Good!

7 Listen and repeat.

/n/	/ŋ/
ca**n**	worki**ng**
	going

8 Listen and repeat. Then put the words in the correct column.

going - screen - song - night - send - meeting

My Turn

9 Think about what you are or aren't going to do tomorrow, this weekend, this summer, after school.

A *What are you going to do this summer?*
B *I'm going to travel abroad.*

one hundred and one **101**

12

1 Listen and read.

The taxi is arriving in ten minutes!

David:	Natalie! Maria! Are you ready to go? The taxi is arriving in ten minutes.
Maria:	Yes, just a minute. We want to say goodbye to everyone.
Natalie:	Bye Sara. See you soon.
Sara:	Bye Natalie. Are you coming back next year?
Natalie:	I hope so!
Jack:	Bye girls! Have a good flight!
Maria and Natalie:	Thanks Jack!
Jack:	Emi wants to say goodbye, too!
Maria and Natalie:	Bye Emi!
Jack:	We're leaving tomorrow. But I'm seeing David next month. We're meeting in Manchester. We're going to a football match together.
Sara:	Don't forget to write.
Natalie:	Don't worry! I'm getting a new computer next week, so I can e-mail you every day and see you on the webcam!
David:	Come on girls! The taxi is here.
Everyone:	Bye! See you soon!

Comprehension

2 Tick (✓) the correct answer.

1 The taxi is arriving in
- A two minutes.
- B ten minutes.
- C twelve minutes.

2 They want to say goodbye to
- A Emi.
- B everyone.
- C Sara.

3 Are Maria and Natalie returning next year?
- A Yes.
- B Maybe.
- C No.

4 Jack and Emi are leaving
- A next week.
- B next month.
- C tomorrow.

5 Who is Jack meeting next month?
- A Sara.
- B Maria.
- C David.

6 What's Natalie getting next week?
- A A computer.
- B A web cam.
- C A car.

Saying Goodbyes

3 Reorder the letters to make words and phrases. Then listen and check.

EBY *bye*

1 ESE OYU ONOS

_____

2 DBGYOEO

_____

3 VEAH A DOGO LGFITH

_____

4 NTDO FERGTO OT RWTIE

_____

102 one hundred and two

12

Communication

Look & Use

We**'re leaving** tomorrow.
Are you **coming** back next year?

5 Work in pairs. Read David's e-mail and ask and answer questions.

> Hi Jack!
> I'm coming to Manchester on Saturday afternoon.
> I'm arriving on the 3.15 train. My friend Jonathan is coming too. We're leaving after the football match.
> I've got three tickets for an open air concert on Saturday evening. We're going with Sara.
> See you on Saturday!
>
> Can you meet us at the station?
> David

What / do / Saturday?
A *What is he doing on Saturday?*
B *He's going to Manchester.*

1 When / arrive?
2 Who / visit?
3 What / do / on Saturday evening?
4 Who / go / with?

6 Work in pairs. Student A: go to page 119. Student B: go to page 121.

Vocabulary

 4 Match the phrases to the pictures. Then listen and check.

<del>go to the cinema</del>   wash dad's car
visit grandpa   go to my friend's party

go to the cinema   1 _____

2 _____   3 _____

My Turn

 7 You are meeting your friend at the weekend. You want to invite him / her to a concert. Write an e-mail telling him / her about your plans.

I'm coming on…
I've got…
I'm arriving…

12 Grammar Focus

going to future

Read the examples and complete the tables.

I'**m going to write** José an e-mail.

Are you **going to tell** José about the weather?

I'**m not going to tell** him about the weather!

Affirmative form			
I	am		watch TV.
You	are		sleep.
He / She / ____	is	going to	play chess.
____ / You / They	____		

Negative form			
I	am not		watch TV.
You	are not		sleep.
He / She / ____	____ not	going to	play chess.
We / You / ____	____ not		

Questions

Are you going to watch TV?
Is he / she / it going to sleep?
Are we / you / they going to play chess?

Short answers

Yes, I am.
No, I'm not.
Yes, he / she / it ____.
No, he / she / it isn't.
Yes, we / you / they are.
No, we / you / they ____.

Look at the examples again and complete the rules.

In the affirmative form the sentence pattern is:

subject + verb _____ + *going to* + _____ form of the main verb.

In the negative and in questions the main verb is always in the base form. We change the verb _____.

We often use *going to* + base form to talk about **intentions** and decisions.

1 Complete Claire's e-mail with *going to* or *not going to* and a verb from the box.

see ~~visit~~ play have sunbathe

Hi Fiona
How are you?
I'm helping Mum at home today, but I'm (1) _going to visit_ my cousin this weekend. We're (2) _____ the new Angelina Jolie film at the cinema and then we're (3) _____ dinner in a Chinese restaurant. She loves Chinese food!
What are you going to do this weekend? Are you going to go to the beach?
It's sunny here, so I'm (4) _____!
But I think I'm (5) _____ tennis with my brother on Sunday.
Well, write soon. I really miss you!
Claire

2 Write some sentences about what you are or aren't going to do in your future life.

go to university   leave school at fifteen
become a pop singer   work in another country
get married and have children   work for my dad

Present continuous for the future

Read the examples and answer the questions.

I'**m waiting** for the taxi at the moment.
We'**re writing** an e-mail now.
They'**re having** a snack right now!

Are these sentences about the present or the future? _____

What are the present time expressions in these sentences?

_____ , _____ , right now.

We can use the present continuous to describe actions that are in progress now.

Read the examples and answer the questions.

The taxi **is arriving** in ten minutes.
I'**m seeing** David next month.
I'**m getting** a new computer next week.

Are these sentences about the present or the future? _____

What are the future time expressions in these sentences?

_____ , _____ , _____ .

We can use the present continuous with a **future** meaning, when we talk about future arrangements or plans.

When we talk about fixed plans, we can use the present continuous + **future time expressions**.

3 Put the present and future time expressions in the right chronological order.

☐ tomorrow   ☐ the day after tomorrow
☐ next week   ☐ now
☒ 1 today   ☐ the week after next
☐ next month ☐ this summer
☐ at the moment ☐ this weekend

4 Do these sentences refer to the present or the future? Write P or F.

I'm meeting my cousins next weekend. _F_
1 She's writing an e-mail. ___
2 They aren't listening to me. ___
3 We're having a big party this summer. ___
4 What are you doing on Sunday afternoon? ___
5 Where's Steve? He's doing his homework. ___

going to vs Present continuous

Read the examples and choose the correct option. Then match the rules to the examples.

1 I'**m going to send** José an e-mail.
2 I'**m getting** a new computer next week.

We use *going to* / *present continuous* when we talk about fixed plans with a definite time.
Sentence no. ____

We use *going to* / *present continuous* when we talk about intentions.
Sentence no. ____

5 Complete the sentences with *going to* or the present continuous.

We'_re meeting_ (meet) James on Sunday evening.
1 I _____ (buy) a new bike with the money I get for my birthday.
2 Laura _____ (arrive) at the hotel at about 7 p.m.
3 My dad _____ (not work) tomorrow. He _____ (play) golf with his friend.
4 Her sister _____ (study) French at university next year.
5 _____ you _____ (go) on holiday this summer?

12 CURIOSITY CORNER

1 Joke Time

Why didn't the skeleton go to the party? Because he had 'nobody' to go with!

2 Wordsearch

Find the five scary Halloween costumes in the wordsearch. Then match the words to the pictures.

witch
vampire
ghost
monster
wizard

1 _____

2 _____

3 _____

4 _____

5 _____

```
A W I T C H T H
A L L G O W E M
W E N H C H I O
I L D O R E N N
Z A S S K T R S
A I C T K O R T
R V A M P I R E
D T R E A T ? R
```

Now use the remaining letters to find the hidden sentence.

__ _____
_____ ___
'_____ __
_____ _,

3 Did you know?

Some supermarkets in Britain are open 24 hours a day!

4 UK Holiday Quiz

Test your festivity knowledge. When do you do these things?

1 Sing songs, called carols, about the birth of Christ.
2 Go to the Notting Hill Carnival in London.
3 Have a fancy dress party and ask people 'trick or treat?'
4 Burn a doll called a 'guy' on a bonfire and watch fireworks.
5 Send cards and give presents to someone you love.
6 Make and eat thin, fried cakes called 'pancakes' with sugar and lemon.

A On Guy Fawkes Night.
B On Pancake Day (or Shrove Tuesday).
C On Valentine's Day.
D At Christmas.
E On August Bank Holiday.
F At Halloween.

106 one hundred and six

CURIOSITY CORNER 12

5. Experiment Time

Cauldron Bubbles

You need
- a clear glass
- water
- oil
- salt

1. Fill a glass half full of water.

2. Add 2 ½ cm of oil. The oil will float on top because it is less dense than the water.

3. Pour in some salt. What can you see?

When you pour in the salt, it brings a bubble of oil down with it. The salt and oil are denser than the water, so they sink.

When the salt dissolves in the water, the oil floats back to the top because it is now less dense than the water.

6. Guess the Meaning

The expression 'shop 'til you drop' means

- ☐ A to dislike shopping
- ☐ B to like shopping
- ☐ C to shop for a long time and feel very tired after shopping

7. Shopaholics

Do you like shopping?

Did you buy anything new last week?

What did you buy?

Some people think the British are a nation of 'shopaholics'. This means they are addicted to shopping. Young people often meet their friends in shopping centres and look around the shops together. They regard shopping as a hobby.

'Bluewater' is Europe's largest shopping centre. It's in Kent in south east England. There are more than 320 shops, 13,000 car park spaces, 40 cafés and restaurants and a 13–screen cinema!

Shops in Britain are usually open Mon-Sat 9 a.m.-5.30 p.m. They are also open on Sundays 10 a.m.-4 p.m. Sunday shopping is very popular.

8. Joke Time

Why did the spider buy a computer?

To surf the Web!

Units 10-12 Check Your Progress

1 Write the name of the activity under each picture.

1 _____ 2 _____ 3 _____

4 _____ 5 _____

5

2 Reorder the jumbled letters to make words about computers.

1 NSNARCE _____
2 NESECR _____
3 DROYEBKA _____
4 PARKEESS _____
5 UEMSO _____
6 RIPRTEN _____

6

3 Find six future time expressions in the wordsnake.

1 _____   4 _____
2 _____   5 _____
3 _____   6 _____

6

4 Complete the list of things that Jessica has to do before her birthday party on Saturday.

Things to do!

make the (1) _n_ _____ions.

buy (2) f____ and (3) _____k.

(4) D_____ the room.

(5) Or_____e the m____c.

make a (6) c_____me.

6

5 Complete the sentences with *going to* or the present continuous.

1 I'm _____ (take) the train at 3 o'clock tomorrow.
2 I want to go shopping – I'm _____ (buy) a scarf for my mum's birthday.
3 I can't play tennis with you tomorrow, I _____ (meet) Sean.
4 I'm _____ (ask) Dad for some money when he comes home.
5 I'm _____ (leave) for Athens on Wednesday.
6 We're _____ (visit) our friends in New York next week.

6

Units 10-12

6 Reorder the conversations and complete them with *can* or *can't*.

A
- [ ] No, you _____!
- [ ] Well, you _____ go but you _____ stay out late. Be home at 10 o'clock.
- [ ] But Andrew _____ go. Why _____ I?
- [ ] Thanks mum!
- [ ] Mum, _____ I go to the rock concert tonight?

B
- [ ] No, you _____ turn right. Turn left at the supermarket and the museum is on the right. You _____ park in the car park.
- [ ] Thank you.
- [ ] Yes, of course. Turn left here and go past the church.
- [ ] Excuse me, _____ you tell me the way to the museum?
- [ ] OK. And _____ I turn right here?

____ / 10

7 Complete the words with *body / one*, *where*, *thing*.

1 Can I get you any_____ at the supermarket?
2 She knew every_____ at the party.
3 We're going some_____ hot on holiday.
4 There was no_____ at home when I called yesterday morning.
5 I've got no_____ to go this weekend.
6 There's some_____ waving at you over there.

____ / 6

8 Complete the sentences.

tired   married   worried   old   dressed up

1 My cat is 9. She's getting _____ now.
2 Laura and Sarah went to a Halloween Fancy Dress party last weekend. They got _____ as witches!!
3 My cousin is getting _____ next Saturday. She's going to Hawaii on her honeymoon!
4 I go to bed at 11 p.m. I always get _____ at this time.
5 My mum always gets _____ when I stay out late.

____ / 5

My final score is: ____ / 50

1 Culture Spot: Roman Britain

1 Read the text and match A-E on the map to the place names.

- [D] Bath
- [ ] London
- [ ] Chester
- [ ] Hadrian's Wall
- [ ] Colchester

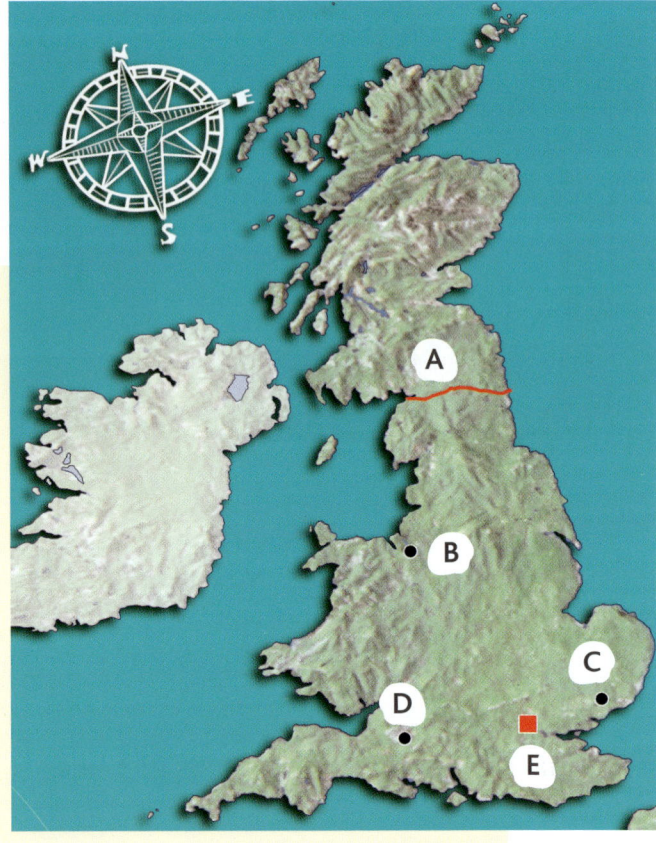

In 55 BC the Roman general Julius Caesar visited Britain. Caesar tried to invade the country but his army was small and the invasion wasn't successful.

In AD 43 the Emperor Claudius returned to Britain with about 40,000 soldiers and invaded the country. He arrived in southern England and conquered Colchester, in the south-east of England.

Between AD 43 and AD 47 the Romans conquered the whole of southern Britain. They founded Londinium around AD 50 and built a bridge across the River Thames. The Romans also conquered Bath in the south-west of England and Chester in the north-west.

Between AD 75 and 77 the Romans conquered the last tribes in the north of the country, making Britain a Roman country. In AD 122 the Emperor Hadrian began building a wall between England and Scotland. It is called 'Hadrian's Wall'. You can walk along parts of the wall today. The Romans remained in Britain from AD 43 to AD 410. That's almost 400 years!

Hot Tip!

BC means *Before Christ*. It refers to a date <u>before</u> the birth of Jesus Christ.
AD means *Anno Domini* in Latin. It refers to a date <u>after</u> the birth of Jesus Christ.

2 Read the text again and tick (✓) T (True) or F (False). Correct the false sentences.

	T	F
1 Julius Caesar had a small army.	☐	☐
2 Emperor Claudius had about 50,000 soldiers.	☐	☐
3 The Romans built a bridge in Chester.	☐	☐
4 Emperor Hadrian didn't build a wall.	☐	☐

3 Now answer the following questions.

1 Where did Emperor Claudius arrive in AD 43?
   _____

2 When did the Romans found Londinium?
   _____

3 Which city did the Romans conquer in the north-west of England?
   _____

4 Where is Hadrian's Wall?
   _____

Interesting Fact

The Romans brought elephants to Britain in AD 43 to frighten the native people!

4 Look at the photos and listen to the four descriptions. Then write the place names.

1 _____
2 _____
3 _____
4 _____

5 Listen to the descriptions again and complete the notes.

Bath
Latin name:
(1) _____.
The Romans built a temple, a (2) _____ and public baths in the city.
The Romans left Bath in (3) _____.

Chester
Chester began as a fort in (4) _____.
Castrum means (5) _____.
Soldiers learnt to (6) _____ in the amphitheatre.

London
The Romans founded London in ___AD 43___.
The city became the capital in (7) _____.
The Romans built a road system and a (8) _____.

Hadrian's Wall
Emperor Hadrian built the wall in the year (9) _____.
It took (10) _____ to build.

Similar or different?

6 What do you know about the history of people of your country? Discuss the following questions with your partner and then complete the text.

1 Who founded the capital city of your country?
2 Are there any famous ancient monuments in your country?
3 What is the most famous monument in your country?
4 Are there any ancient monuments in your town?
5 Who built them and when?

Legend says that _____ was founded by _____.

In _____ you can see _____ famous ancient monuments.

The most famous monument is _____.

In my town there is _____
_____.

2 Culture Spot: Cities, Towns and Villages

1 Look at the map and complete the table below.

The British Isles

Capital cities		
England		London
Scotland	1	_____
Wales	2	_____
Northern Ireland	3	_____
Republic of Ireland	4	_____

Other important cities		
Birmingham		
1 _____		4 _____
2 _____		5 _____
3 _____		6 _____

2 Read what Joe and Annie say about where they live. Find:

1 two differences
2 one thing they have in common

My name's Joe and I live in Birmingham. It is often considered to be the second most important city of the United Kingdom.
There are museums, theatres, restaurants, shops, parks and cinemas.
It's a very lively city and there's always something happening! Sometimes the traffic and pollution can be a problem. We've got two football teams: Aston Villa and Birmingham City. They're two of the oldest teams in the UK!

Hi, my name's Annie and I live in Stratford-upon-Avon. It's a small quiet market town in England but a lot of tourists visit it because it's the birthplace of William Shakespeare.
I like living here – there's always something to do. On Saturdays, I usually look around the market with my friends.
There's very little traffic so it's a really relaxing and healthy place to live.

Llanfairpwllgwyngyllgogerychwyrndrobwllllantysiliogogogoch

 3 Now listen to Rhys. Then match the two parts of the sentences.

    E   Rhys lives in a village on
1 ☐ The village has
2 ☐ Rhys thinks the countryside is
3 ☐ The village hasn't got a cinema and there aren't
4 ☐ In the evenings there aren't any

A many shops.
B beautiful.
C buses.
D the longest place name in Britain.
E the Isle of Anglesey.

4 Read the text and answer the questions.

The United Kingdom has a population of about 60 million people. Most people live in the big urban and suburban areas between London and Manchester. In fact, approximately 80% of people in England live in an urban environment and less than 7% live in rural villages. The Republic of Ireland has a population of about 4 million. Around 60% of the population live in urban areas.

In the UK, a city is a large and important settlement with a charter (a legal document) from the monarch. When a town receives a 'Royal Charter' it becomes a city. Most cities in the U.K. have a cathedral.
There are currently 66 official cities in the UK: 50 in England, 5 in Wales, 6 in Scotland and 5 in Northern Ireland.

A town is traditionally a settlement with a 'town charter' from the monarch. A town is larger than a village but smaller than a city. There is usually a marketplace.

A village is a place where there are at least 20 buildings. There must be at least one public building such as a church, a school or a post office. There are over 10,000 villages in Britain.

1. How many people live in the UK?
2. Where do most people live in the UK?
3. How many people live in the Republic of Ireland?
4. How many official cities are there in Wales?
5. What does a town usually have?
6. What buildings can you see in a village?

Interesting Fact

A small village without a church is called a 'hamlet'.

Similar or different?

5 What do you know about the cities, towns and villages in your country? Discuss the following questions with your partner. Then complete the text.

1. What's the population of your country?
2. What are the most important cities in your country?
3. Do you live in a city, a town or a village?
4. What buildings are there in the place where you live?
5. What differences are there between life in the countryside and life in the city?
6. Where would you prefer to live? Why?

I live in _____.
The country's population is _____.
The most important cities in my country are _____
_____.
In my city / town / village there is _____
_____
_____.

3 Culture Spot — British History Timeline

1 Look at the pictures and read the texts. Then choose and write the correct caption below each picture.

The Vikings   Battle of Hastings   Henry VIII
Industrial Revolution   Winston Churchill

In the beginning of history there were no nations in the British Isles. Unity came from conquests.

The **Romans** conquered southern Britain between AD 43 and AD 47. In AD 410 they left Britain to defend Rome. The civilisation they brought to Britain had a lasting effect. Roman buildings and roads can be found all over the country.
In AD 450 the **Anglo-Saxons** successfully invaded England. They came from Germany, Denmark and The Netherlands. They ruled for about 500 years.
The **Vikings** arrived from Scandinavia between 700 and 1000. They were great travellers and sailed on long ships. Following fierce battles, the Vikings conquered a large part of England.

1 _____

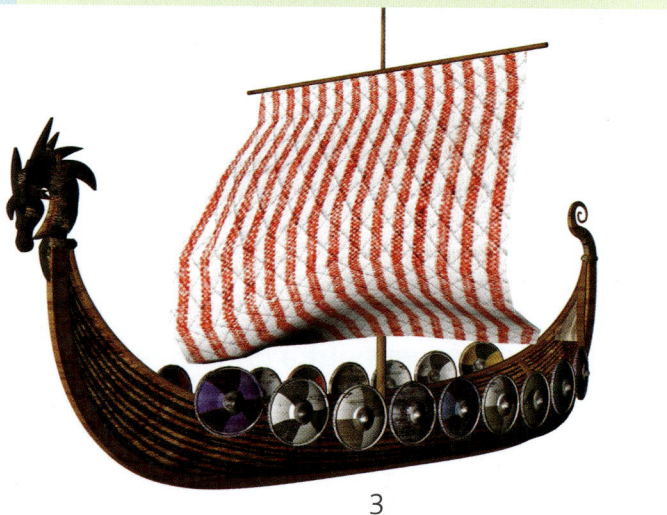

2 _____

The **Normans** conquered England in 1066. William, Duke of Normandy sailed from France to England. He defeated King Harold of England at the **Battle of Hastings** in 1066. It is the most famous battle in English history. He was crowned king and became known as William the Conqueror.

The **Tudors** ruled England and Wales from 1485-1603. Henry VIII was a famous Tudor king. He married six times and beheaded two of his wives!
In 1534 Henry VIII broke from the Roman Catholic Church. He wanted a divorce from Catherine of Aragon, but the Pope refused to annul his marriage. England became a Protestant country.

3 _____

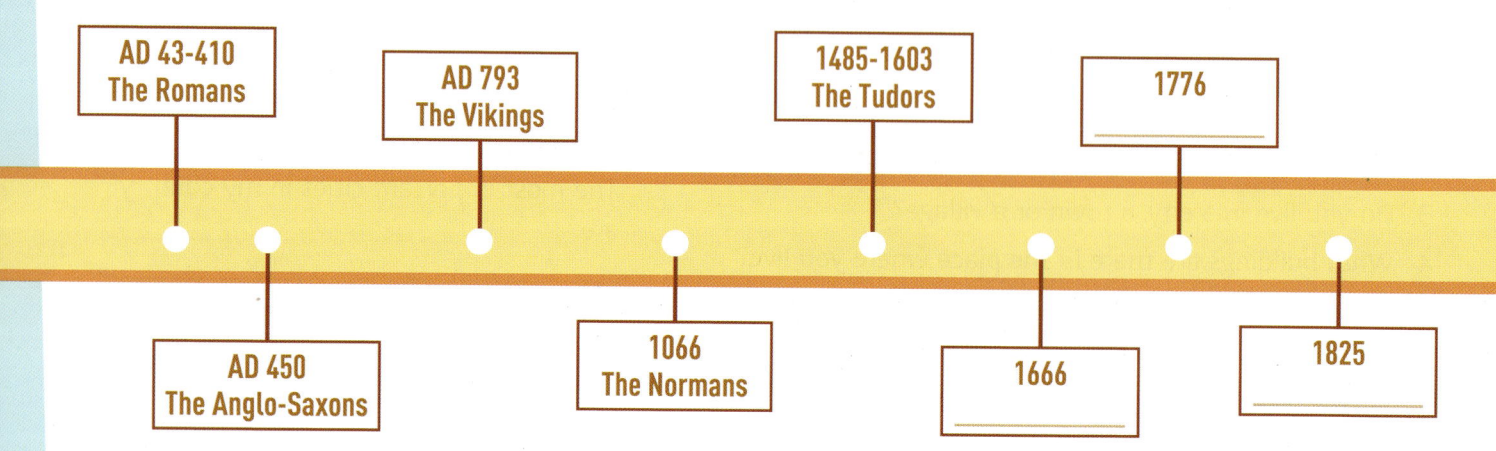

Interesting Fact

The Victorians invented the police force.

4 _____

Victoria was crowned queen in 1837 when she was 18 years old. She reigned until her death in 1901. During the **Victorian Times** Britain built a huge empire and became the most powerful country in the world. **The Industrial Revolution** (1750-1850) changed Britain in many ways. It became the first industrial nation in the world. Factories were built and villages grew into towns.

At the beginning of Queen Victoria's reign, only rich children went to school. Children from poor families worked all day in factories. In 1870 the **Education Act** was passed. It offered schools for all children between the age of 5 and 12.

During **World War II** (1939-1945) London and other cities in England were frequently bombed. Children in Britain were sent out of the cities and were evacuated to the countryside. In 1940 Winston Churchill became Prime Minister. For many people he was the symbol of Britain.

In 1973 Britain became a member of the **European Economic Community** (now European Union, EU).

5 _____

2 Read the texts in exercise 1 again. Then read the following sentences and tick (✓) T (True) or F (False). Correct the false sentences.

	T	F
The Romans conquered Britain between AD 40 and AD 42.	☐	✓

No, the Romans conquered Britain between AD 43 and AD 47.

1 The Anglo-Saxons came from France. ☐ ☐
2 The Battle of Hastings was in 1055. ☐ ☐
3 Henry VIII married eight times. ☐ ☐
4 Victoria became queen when she was 18 years old. ☐ ☐
5 During the Industrial Revolution many factories were built. ☐ ☐
6 The Education Act was passed in 1860. ☐ ☐

C 2.55

3 When did these historic events take place? Write them on the timeline. Then listen and check.

The world's **first railway** opens in Britain.

The **Great Fire** of London.

The United States **Declaration of Independence** from Great Britain.

Sir Berners-Lee invents the **WWW** (World Wide Web).

Similar or different?

4 What do you know about the history of your country? Discuss the following questions with your partner.

1 Did anyone invaded your country in past centuries?
2 Who was the most famous monarch or political leader of your country?
3 What dates are important for the history of your country? Why?

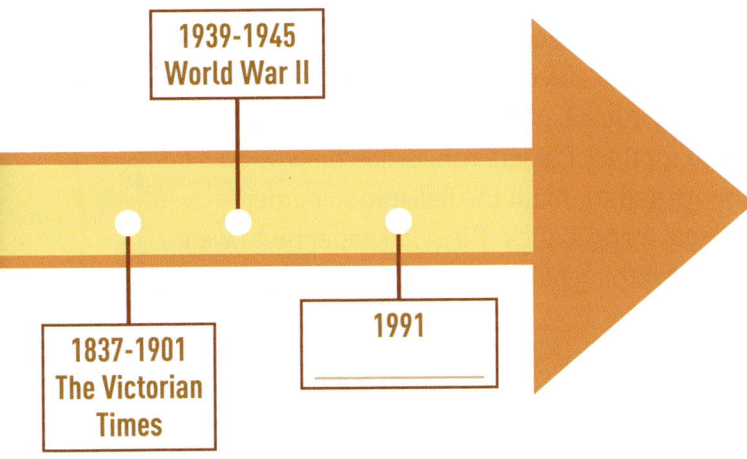

1939-1945 World War II

1991

1837-1901 The Victorian Times

4 Culture Spot

Sports in the English-Speaking World

1 British and American students play lots of sports at school. P.E. (Physical Education) lessons are compulsory. Look at the photos and read the descriptions. Then write the name of the sport below the correct photo.

badminton   baseball
netball   basketball
cricket   hockey   rugby

1 _____
This is the national sport of the United States.

2 _____
A sport played traditionally by girls at school in the U.K. You play outside on a grass pitch.

3 _____
This sport is very popular in the U.K., India and Pakistan.

2 Read about four sports that British and American teenagers play. Write the name of the sport above each description.

A _____

This is a game played especially in the US. There are two teams of nine players. One team throws a small ball and the other team tries to hit it with a bat. The field is called a 'diamond'. Teams get points by running and touching 'bases' before the other team can return the ball. The *New York Yankees* is a famous team.

B _____

This is a game played by two teams of five players. It was invented in America in 1891. Players get points by throwing a large ball into a hoop (the basket). You get more points for scoring depending on where you shoot from – the further away, the more points you get. The ball is moved around by bouncing it between teammates.

C _____

This sport is similar to tennis. Players hit a shuttlecock across a net using a racket. A shuttlecock is a small light kind of ball, originally with feathers around it. People usually play this sport indoors.

D _____

Girls at school in the UK often play this sport. There are two teams of eleven players. Players use curved sticks and a small hard ball. The rules are quite similar to football. Players run, tackle their opponents and try to hit the ball into the other team's goal using a stick. The goalkeeper must wear protective clothing because the ball is very hard!

4 _____
A racket sport played either as singles (2 players) or doubles (4 players).

5 _____
A team sport played mainly by girls.

6 _____
This sport was invented in the U.K. but the most famous team is the 'All Blacks' from New Zealand.

7 _____
This sport is popular all around the world.

3 Read the texts again and answer the questions.
1. What is a baseball field called?
2. In which sport do you hit a shuttlecock?
3. Do people usually play badminton indoors or outdoors?
4. How many teams are there in a game of basketball?
5. What equipment do you use in the game of hockey?
6. What must the goalkeeper wear in the game of hockey?

4 C 2.56 Listen to James, a 13 year old student from Oxford, talking about P.E. lessons and Sports Day in a British school. Tick (✓) T (True) or F (False).

	T	F
1 James's favourite subject is P.E.	☐	☐
2 He has 3 P.E. lessons each week.	☐	☐
3 In winter the boys play basketball.	☐	☐
4 In spring the girls play hockey.	☐	☐
5 Every winter James's school organises a Sports Day.	☐	☐
6 James goes to a tennis club on Thursdays.	☐	☐

Interesting Fact

In Australian Rules Football, players can use their hands to pass the ball.

Similar or different?

5 What do you know about sports in your country? Discuss the following questions with your partner and then complete the text.

1. What sports do you play at school?
2. How often do you do them?
3. What's your favourite sport?
4. Do girls and boys play different sports?
5. Do you know any famous sportsmen / women in your country?
6. What do they play?

My school is called _____. At school we play _____.
My favourite sport is _____.
The girls play _____ and the boys play _____.
Some famous sportsmen / women are _____
_____
_____.

one hundred and seventeen **117**

Interactive pages

Unit 2, page 17 - exercise 5

Student B
Look at your map of the British Isles. Listen to Student A and draw the correct weather symbols on the cities. Then look at your map and read the weather forecast to Student A.

Today it's windy in Swansea...

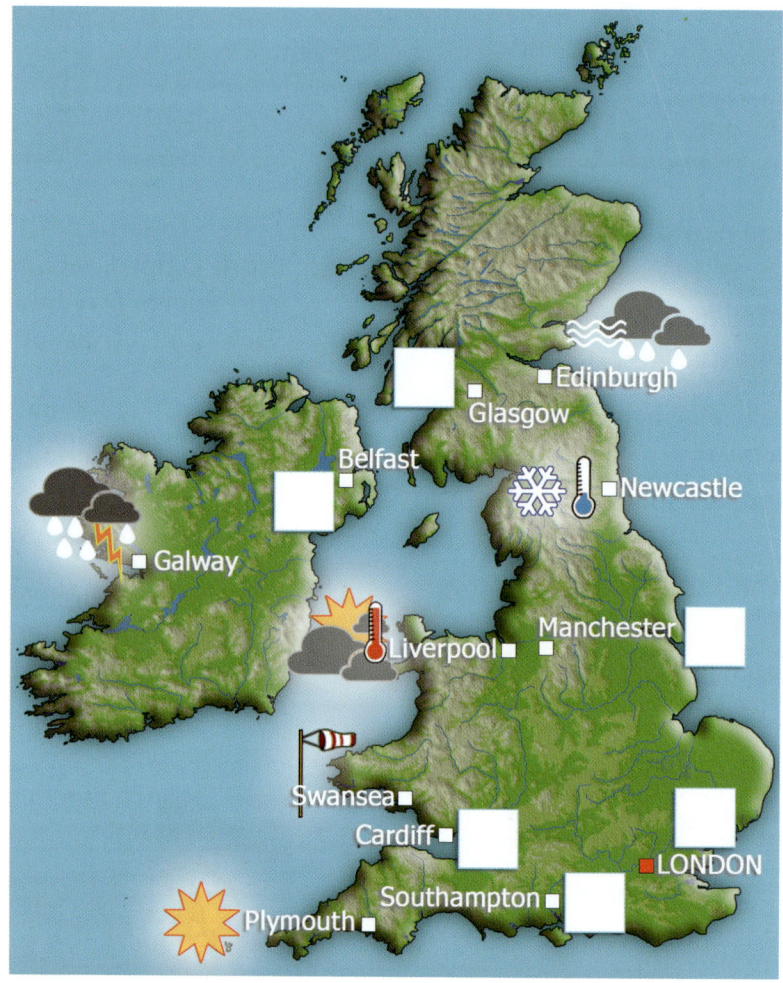

Unit 3, page 25 - exercise 5

Student A
You are a famous actor / actress and your partner is a rockstar. Answer your partner's questions. Then swap roles.

Your passport

B *Where were you on 25th October 2005?*
A *I was in Australia.*

Your partner's passport

A *When were you in Brazil?*
B *I was in Brazil on…*

Unit 12, page 103 - exercise 6

Student A
The school holidays start next week. Look at your diary and ask and answer questions to find a day when you are both free to meet.

Monday 8th	go swimming with Anna
Tuesday 9th	play volleyball
Wednesday 10th	
Thursday 11th	go to the cinema with Rachel
Friday 12th	
Saturday 13th	Meet Sam and John
Sunday 14th	visit Aunt Laura

A *What are you doing on Monday?*
B *I'm going swimming with Anna.*

one hundred and nineteen 119

Interactive pages

Unit 3, page 25 - exercise 5

Student B
You are a famous rockstar and your partner is an actor / actress. Ask your partner questions. Then swap roles.

Your partner's passport

B *Where were you on 25th October 2005?*
A *I was in ...*

Your passport

A *When were you in Brazil?*
B *I was in Brazil on 23rd February 2007.*

Unit 5, page 43 - exercise 7

Ask and answer questions. Then swap roles.

A Say hello to your partner and welcome him / her.
B Thank your partner.
A Ask where he / she went on holiday.
B Answer.
A Ask what he / she saw.
B Answer.
A Ask if he / she sent you a postcard.
B Answer.

A *Hi Mark, welcome back!*
B *Hi Julie.*
A *Where did you go on holiday?*
B *I went to ...*

Unit 11, page 95 - exercise 7

Student B
Look at the picture below.
Ask and answer questions about the picture.

A *Is anybody dancing in your picture?*
B *No, nobody is dancing.*

A *Is anybody drinking?*
B *Yes, somebody is drinking.*

Unit 12, page 103 - exercise 6

Student B
The school holidays start next week.
Look at your diary and ask and answer questions to find a day when you are both free to meet.

Monday 8th	visit grandpa
Tuesday 9th	play basketball
Wednesday 10th	go shopping with Laura
Thursday 11th	
Friday 12th	
Saturday 13th	go to Lucy's party
Sunday 14th	wash dad's car

A *What are you doing on Monday?*
B *I'm visiting my grandfather on Monday.*

Glossary

Unit 1
athletics /æθˈletɪcs/
basketball /ˈbɑːskɪbɔːl/
best friend /best frend/
board games /bɔːd geɪm/
boring /ˈbɔːrɪŋ/
canoeing /kəˈnuːɪŋ/
climbing /ˈklaɪmɪŋ/
cycling /ˈsaɪklɪŋ/
exciting /ɪkˈsaɪtɪŋ/
gymnastics /dʒɪmˈnæstɪks/
happen (v) /ˈhæpən/
hard /hɑːd/
hate /heɪt/
horse riding /hɔːs raɪdɪŋ/
last /lɑːst/
martial arts /ˈmɑːʃəl ɑːts/
rock /rɑk/
rollerblading /ˈrəʊləbleɪdɪŋ/
running about /rʌnɪŋ əˈbaʊt/
sailing /ˈseɪlɪŋ/
scary /ˈskeəri/
science fiction /saɪəns ˈfɪkʃən/
snowboarding /ˈsnəʊbɔːdɪŋ/
take photos /teɪk ˈfəʊtəʊs/
thriller /ˈθrɪlə/
tiring /ˈtaɪərɪŋ/
tomatoes /təˈmɑːtəʊs/
too much /tuː mʌtʃ/
town /taʊn/
treasure hunt /ˈtreʒə hʌnt/
water polo /ˈwɔːtə ˈpəʊləʊ/
Well done! /wel dʌn/
windsurfing /ˈwɪndsɜːfɪŋ/
winter sport /ˈwɪntə spɔːt/

Unit 2
adverb of manner /ˈædvɜːb əv ˈmænə/
badly /ˈbædli/
boring /ˈbɔːrɪŋ/
carefully /ˈkeəfli/
carelessly /ˈkeələsli/
chance /tʃɑːns/
change (v) /tʃeɪndʒ/
cloudy /ˈklaʊdi/
clumsily /ˈklʌmzɪli/
comfort (v) /ˈkʌmfət/
dangerous /ˈdeɪndʒərəs/
destination /ˌdestɪˈneɪʃn/
draw (v) /drɔː/
drive (v) /draɪv/
driving licence /ˈdraɪvɪŋ ˈlaɪsəns/
dry (v) /draɪ/
expensive /ɪkˈspensɪv/
fall over (v) /fɔːl ˈəʊvə/
foggy /ˈfɒgi/
go and visit (v) /gəʊ ənd ˈvɪzɪt/
Guess what? /ges wɒt/
guest /gest/
happen (v) /ˈhæpən/
happily /ˈhæpɪli/
hard /hɑːd/
hot and sunny /hɒt ənd ˈsʌni/
I can't stand… /aɪ kɑːnt stænd/
indoors /ɪnˈdɔːz/
lightning /ˈlaɪtnɪŋ/
line /laɪn/
loudly /ˈlaʊdli/
Lucky thing! /ˈlʌki θɪŋ/
miss (v) /mɪs/
never /ˈnevə/
of course /əv kɔːs ‖ ɒv/
pair /peə/
picture /ˈpɪktʃə/
plan (v) /plæn/
quickly /ˈkwɪkli/
rain (v) /reɪn/
sadly /ˈsædli/
silly /ˈsɪli/
slowly /ˈsləʊli/
snow (v) /snəʊ/
stormy /ˈstɔːmi/
tail /teɪl/
thunder /ˈθʌndə/
trip /trɪp/
wag (v) /wæg/
wait (v) /weɪt/
walk (v) /wɔːk/
warm /wɔːm/
weather forecast /ˈweðə ˈfɔːkɑːst/
well /wel/
wet /wet/
windy /ˈwɪndi/
wonder (v) /ˈwʌndə/

CLIL - Computer Safety
aching wrist /ˈeɪkɪŋ rɪst/
against the law /əˈgenst ðə lɔː/
hurt (v) /hɜːt/
keep (v) /kiːp/
remedy /ˈremədi/
straight /streɪt/

Unit 3
5 years ago /faɪv jɪəz əˈgəʊ/
a long time ago /ə lɒŋ taɪm əˈgəʊ/
actor /ˈæktə/
actually /ˈæktʃəli/
amazing /əˈmeɪzɪŋ/
April fool /ˈeɪprəl fuːl/
architect /ˈɑːkɪtekt/
autumn /ˈɔːtəm/
be born (v) /biː bɔːn/
birthday /ˈbɜːθdeɪ/
called /kɔːld/
dancer /ˈdɑːnsə/
doctor /ˈdɒktə/
early /ˈɜːli/
interesting /ˈɪntrəstɪŋ/
job /dʒɒb/
last month /lɑːst mʌnθ/
last week /lɑːst wiːk/
last year /lɑːst jɪə/
lawyer /ˈlɔːjə/
library /ˈlaɪbrəri/
month /mʌnθ/

Glossary

opening /ˈəʊp(ə)nɪŋ/
ordinal numbers /ˈɔːdɪnəl ˈnʌmbəz/
pilot /ˈpaɪlət/
place /pleɪs/
real /rɪəl/
sandy /ˈsændi/
season /ˈsiːzən/
singer /ˈsɪŋə/
someone /ˈsʌmwʌn/
spring /sprɪŋ/
stamp /stæmp/
summer /ˈsʌmə/
teacher /ˈtiːtʃə/
today /təˈdeɪ/
tour guide /tʊə ‖ tɔː gaɪd/
What's the matter? /wɒts ðə ˈmætə/
white beach /waɪt biːtʃ/
winter /ˈwɪntə/
yesterday /ˈjestədeɪ/

Unit 3 - Curiosity Corner

aged /eɪdʒd ‖ ˈeɪdʒɪd/
cut the grass (v) /kʌt ðə grɑːs/
earn (v) /ɜːn/
enemy /ˈenəmi/
even more /ˈiːvn mɔː/
general knowledge /ˈdʒenrəl ˈnɒlɪdʒ/
go for a spin (v) /gəʊ fə(r) ə spɪn/
a great deal of /ə greɪt diːl əv/
ill /ɪl/
knowledge /ˈnɒlɪdʒ/
odd job /ɒd dʒɒb/
paper round /ˈpeɪpə raʊnd/
pocket money /ˈpɒkɪt ˈmʌni/
ship /ʃɪp/
shop assistant /ʃɒp əˈsɪst(ə)nt/
side /saɪd/
silver /ˈsɪlvə/
spin (v) /spɪn/
stand up to (v) /stænd ʌp tə/
waiter /ˈweɪtə/
waitress /ˈweɪtrəs/

World Cup /wɜːld kʌp/

Unit 4

act (v) /ækt/
actress /ˈæktrəs/
again /əˈgen/
arrive (v) /əˈraɪv/
billions /ˈbɪljənz ‖ bɪlɪjənz/
by train /baɪ treɪn/
carry (v) /ˈkæri/
charity /ˈtʃærɪti/
chat (v) /tʃæt/
countryside /ˈkʌntriˌsaɪd/
die (v) /daɪ/
documentary series /ˌdɒkjʊˈment(ə)ri ˈsɪəriːz/
drama /ˈdrɑːmə/
Earth /ɜːθ/
everywhere /ˈevriweə/
far away /fɑː əˈweɪ/
find out (v) /faɪnd aʊt/
fit (v) /fɪt/
get together (v) /get təˈgeðə/
heavy /ˈhevi/
hundreds /ˈhʌndrədz/
interview /ˈɪntəvjuː/
journalist /ˈdʒɜːnəlɪst/
journey /ˈdʒɜːni/
know (v) /neʊ/
learn (v) /lɜːn/
major /ˈmeɪdʒə/
marathon /ˈmærəθən/
medical treatment /ˈmedɪkl ˈtriːtmənt/
mile /maɪl/
miss (v) /mɪs/
motorcycle trip /ˈməʊtəˌsaɪkl trɪp/
nanny /ˈnæni/
nearly /ˈnɪəli/
orphanage /ˈɔːf(ə)nɪdʒ/
paint (v) /peɪnt/
play cards (v) /pleɪ kɑːdz/

practise (v) /ˈpræktɪs/
raise money (v) /reɪz ˈmʌni/
remember (v) /rɪˈmembə/
slow /sləʊ/
spend (v) /spend/
stay up (v) /steɪ ʌp/
stop (v) /stɒp/
suitcase /ˈsuːtkeɪs/
survival training /səˈvaɪvl ˈtreɪnɪŋ/
switch on (v) /swɪtʃ ɒn/
team up (v) /tiːm ʌp/
tent /tent/
thousands /ˈθaʊzndz/
train (v) /treɪn/
travel (v) /ˈtrævl/
wedding /ˈwedɪŋ/

Unit 5

amazing /əˈmeɪzɪŋ/
art gallery /ɑːt ˈgæləri/
become (v) /bɪˈkʌm/
bring (v) /brɪŋ/
buy (v) /baɪ/
castle /ˈkɑːsl/
ceiling /ˈsiːlɪŋ/
clever /ˈklevə/
coin /kɔɪn/
design (v) /dɪˈzaɪn/
dome /dəʊm/
dream /driːm/
Emperor /ˈemp(ə)rə/
everyone /ˈevriwʌn/
famous /ˈfeɪməs/
fight (v) /faɪt/
fly (v) /flaɪ/
forget (v) /fəˈget/
fountain /ˈfaʊntɪn/
gladiator /ˈglædiˌeɪtə/
ham /hæm/
leave (v) /liːv/
make a cake (v) /meɪk ə keɪk/
make a wish (v) /meɪk ə wɪʃ/

Glossary

mean (v) /miːn/
mind /maɪnd/
mine /maɪn/
more /mɔː/
need (v) /niːd/
Pope /pəʊp/
postcard /ˈpəʊstˌkɑːd/
put (v) /pʊt/
receive (v) /rəˈsiːv/
sculpture /ˈskʌlptʃə/
self-portrait /self ˈpɔːtrɪt/
send (v) /send/
sightseeing /ˈsaɪtˌsiːɪŋ/
Spanish Steps /ˈspænɪʃ steps/
statue /ˈstætʃuː/
than /ðən ‖ ðæn/
the late 1960s /ðə leɪt ˈnaɪntiːn ˈsɪkstiz/
throw (v) /θrəʊ/
thumbs down /θʌmz daʊn/
thumbs up /θʌmz ʌp/
tomato sauce /təˈmɑːtəʊ sɔːs/
try (v) /traɪ/
tuna /ˈtjuːnə/
welcome back /ˈwelkəm bæk/

CLIL - Discovering Food

anti-ageing /ˈænti ˈeɪdʒɪŋ/
bean /biːn/
dry (v) /draɪ/
fatigue /fəˈtiːg/
heat (v) /hiːt/
in search of /ɪn sɜːtʃ əv/
melt (v) /melt/
mould /məʊld/
peanuts /ˈpiːˌnʌts/
pick (v) /pɪk/
pour (v) /pɔː/
pumpkin /ˈpʌmpkɪn/
ripe /raɪp/
trip /trɪp/
wrap (v) /ræp/

Unit 6

across /əˈkrɒs/
bank /bæŋk/
border /ˈbɔːdə/
building /ˈbɪldɪŋ/
bus stop /bʌs stɒp/
by ferry /baɪ ˈferi/
by plane /baɪ pleɪn/
church /tʃɜːtʃ/
cinema /ˈsɪnəmə/
coach /kəʊtʃ/
deep /diːp/
department store /dɪˈpɑːtmənt stɔː/
down /daʊn/
go past (v) /gəʊ pɑːst/
guidebook /ˈgaɪdbʊk/
high /haɪ/
hospital /ˈhɒspɪtl/
I think so. /aɪ θɪŋk səʊ/
into /ˈɪntə, ˈɪntʊ, ˈɪntuː/
long /lɒŋ/
on foot /ɒn fʊt/
over /ˈəʊvə/
panic (v) /ˈpænɪk/
police station /pəˈliːs ˈsteɪʃn/
railway station /ˈreɪlweɪ ˈsteɪʃn/
restaurant /ˈrest(ə)rɒnt/
roundabout /ˈraʊndəˌbaʊt/
say goodbye /seɪ gʊdˈbaɪ/
school /skuːl/
straight ahead /streɪt əˈhed/
supermarket /ˈsuːpəˌmɑːkɪt/
take (v) /teɪk/
tall /tɔːl/
tell the way (v) /tel ðə weɪ/
the right way /ðə raɪt weɪ/
through /θruː/
top floor /tɒp flɔː/
towards /təˈwɔːdz/
traffic light /ˈtræfɪk laɪt/
turn left (v) /tɜːn left/
turn right (v) /tɜːn raɪt/
under /ˈʌndə/
up /ʌp/
wide /waɪd/
wrong /rɒŋ/

Unit 6 - Curiosity Corner

age /eɪdʒ/
bright red /braɪt red/
busy /ˈbɪzi/
Channel Tunnel /ˈtʃænəl ˈtʌnəl/
deliver (v) /dəˈlɪvə/
dig (v) /dɪg/
parcel /ˈpɑːsl/
riddle /ˈrɪdl/
stamp /stæmp/

Unit 7

a bit /ə bɪt/
any kind /ˈeni kaɪnd/
as... as /əz .... əz/
bad /bæd/
bat /bæt/
better /ˈbetə/
bird /bɜːd/
blind as a bat /blaɪnd əz ə bæt/
blind /blaɪnd/
brilliant /ˈbrɪljənt/
busy /ˈbɪzi/
by boat /baɪ bəʊt/
chatty /ˈtʃæti/
cheap /tʃiːp/
cheerful /ˈtʃɪəfl/
clean /kliːn/
cold /kəʊld/
Come on! /kʌm ɒn/
cool as a cucumber /kuːl əz ə ˈkjuːˌkʌmbə/
cucumber /ˈkjuːˌkʌmbə/
dark /dɑːk/
decide (v) /dɪˈsaɪd/
delicious /dɪˈlɪʃəs/
dirty /ˈdɜːti/

Glossary

dry /draɪ/
easy /ˈiːzi/
ecological /iːkəˈlɒdʒɪkl/
everybody else /ˈevrɪˌbɒdi els/
exciting /ɪkˈsaɪtɪŋ/
extrovert /ˈekstrəˌvɜːt/
fast /fɑːst/
feather /ˈfeðə/
flash /flæʃ/
food /fuːd/
free as a bird /friː əz ə bɜːd/
free /friː/
friendly /ˈfrendli/
give up (v) /gɪv ʌp/
good /gʊd/
handsome /ˈhæns(ə)m/
healthy /ˈhelθi/
hear (v) /hɪə/
I can't wait. /aɪ kɑːnt weɪt/
ice /aɪs/
Let me show you. /let miː ʃəʊ juː/
light /laɪt/
moody /ˈmuːdi/
mountain /ˈmaʊntɪn/
near /nɪə/
nice /naɪs/
noisy /ˈnɔɪzi/
NYC /en waɪ siː/
optimistic /ˌɒptɪˈmɪstɪk/
patient /ˈpeɪʃənt/
poor /pʊə ll pɔː/
pretty /ˈprɪti/
quiet /ˈkwaɪət/
relaxing /rəˈlæksɪŋ/
rich /rɪtʃ/
safe /seɪf/
sea /siː/
seaside /ˈsiːˌsaɪd/
sensible /ˈsensəbl/
sensitive /ˈsensətɪv/
shop /ʃɒp/

short /ʃɔːt/
shy /ʃaɪ/
slippery /ˈslɪpəri/
slow /sləʊ/
small /smɔːl/
snake /sneɪk/
stand (v) /stænd/
strong /strɒŋ/
such a /sʌtʃ ə/
suppose (v) /səˈpəʊz/
take no notice (v) /teɪk nəʊ ˈnəʊtɪs/
thin /θɪn/
very handy /ˈveri ˈhændi/
wet /wet/
worse /wɜːs/

Unit 8

agree (v) /əˈgriː/
available /əˈveɪl(ə)bl/
basic /ˈbeɪsɪk/
beside /bɪˈsaɪd/
crazy /ˈkreɪzi/
definitely /ˈdef(ə)nətli/
detail /ˈdiːteɪl/
ever /ˈevə/
find (v) /faɪnd/
lake /leɪk/
leaflet /ˈliːflət/
miniature /ˈmɪnətʃə/
monument /ˈmɒnjʊmənt/
mosquito /mɒˈskiːtəʊ/
in-flight services /ɪn flaɪt ˈsɜːvɪsɪz/
opera house /ˈɒp(ə)rə haʊs/
present /ˈpreznt/
provide with (v) /prəˈvaɪd wɪð/
river /ˈrɪvə/
scary /ˈskeəri/
so far /səʊ fɑː/
swot /swɒt/
the best /ðə best/
the furthest /ðə ˈfɜːðɪst/
the worst /ðə wɜːst/

thing /θɪŋ/
to be trained (v) /treɪnd/
tower /ˈtaʊə ll ˈtaʊwə/
whose /huːz/
wood /wʊd/

CLIL – Electricity and Lightning

charged /tʃɑːdʒd/
crowded /ˈkraʊdɪd/
drop (v) /drɒp/
electrical charge /ɪˈlektrɪkl tʃɑːdʒ/
kite /kaɪt/
light bulb /laɪt bʌlb/
lightning /ˈlaɪtnɪŋ/
low /ləʊ/
shed /ʃed/
unless /ənˈles/
washing line /ˈwɒʃɪŋ laɪn/
wire fence /waɪə fens/

Unit 9

bandstand /ˈbændˌstænd/
be quiet /bi ˈkwaɪət/
begin (v) /bɪˈgɪn/
behind /bɪˈhaɪnd/
bench /bentʃ/
between /bɪˈtwiːn/
boating area /ˈbəʊtɪŋ ˈeərɪə/
cooker /ˈkʊkə/
cross (v) /krɒs/
door /dɔː/
drop (v) /drɒp/
feeling /ˈfiːlɪŋ/
finally /ˈfaɪnəli/
first /fɜːst/
flower bed /ˈflaʊə bed/
fridge /frɪdʒ/
get ready (v) /get ˈredi/
headmaster /ˌhedˈmɑːstə/
heart /hɑːt/
hold (v) /həʊld/
ice cream van /aɪs kriːm væn/
in front of /ɪn frʌnt əv/

Glossary

in the middle /ɪn ðə mɪdl/
in /ɪn/
jog (v) /dʒɒg/
lead /liːd/
line /laɪn/
lipstick /ˈlɪpˌstɪk/
make-up artist /meɪk ʌp ˈɑːtɪst/
mirror /ˈmɪrə/
next to /nekst tuː ‖ tə/
on /ɒn/
opposite /ˈɒpəsɪt/
over there /ˈəʊvə ðeə/
rescuer /ˈreskjuːə/
rubbish bin /ˈrʌbɪʃ bɪn/
seat /siːt/
sink /sɪŋk/
sit (v) /sɪt/
sofa-bed /ˈsəʊfə bed/
suddenly /ˈsʌdnli/
sunbathe (v) /ˈsʌnˌbeɪð/
sunglasses /ˈsʌnˌglɑːsɪz/
table /ˈteɪbl/
then, next /ðen/ /nekst/
turn around (v) /tɜːn əˈraʊnd/
wardrobe /ˈwɔːdrəʊb/
You're welcome. /jɔː ˈwelkəm/

Unit 9 - Curiosity Corner

believe (v) /bəˈliːv/
bird /bɜːd/
blush (v) /blʌʃ/
brave /breɪv/
colour-blind /ˈkʌlə blaɪnd/
football pitch /ˈfʊtbɔːl pɪtʃ/
fox /fɒks/
hummingbird /ˈhʌmɪŋˌbɜːd/
kitten /ˈkɪtn/
length /leŋθ/
lion /ˈlaɪən/
mosquito /mɒˈskiːtəʊ/
peacock /ˈpiːkɒk/
playful /ˈpleɪfl/

proud /praʊd/
rabbit /ˈræbɪt/
salad dressing /ˈsæləd ˈdresɪŋ/
sly /slaɪ/
snail /sneɪl/
snake /sneɪk/

Unit 10

2 euros each /tuː ˈjʊərəʊz iːtʃ/
beat (v) /biːt/
birth /bɜːθ/
borrow (v) /ˈbɒrəʊ/
bug /bʌg/
caveman /ˈkeɪvˌmæn/
chess /tʃes/
conservation /ˌkɒnsəˈveɪʃən/
cycle up (v) /saɪkl ʌp/
dark ride /dɑːk raɪd/
discover (v) /dɪˈskʌvə/
find (v) /faɪnd/
get to (v) /get tuː ‖ tə/
get the bus (v) /get ðə bʌs/
give right of way (v) /gɪv raɪt əv weɪ/
hike (v) /haɪk/
join (v) /dʒɔɪn/
keep busy (v) /kiːp ˈbɪzi/
kingdom /ˈkɪŋdəm/
lake /leɪk/
leave (v) /liːv/
lend (v) /lend/
live show /laɪv ʃəʊ/
lots more /lɒts mɔː/
midnight /ˈmɪdˌnaɪt/
monster /ˈmɒnstə/
motion simulator /ˈməʊʃn ˈsɪmjʊˌleɪtə/
nearly /ˈnɪəli/
neighbour /ˈneɪbə/
No entry /nəʊ ˈentri/
No left turn /nəʊ left tɜːn/
No parking /nəʊ ˈpɑːkɪŋ/
No right turn /nəʊ raɪt tɜːn/
One-way /wʌn weɪ/

overtake (v) /ˌəʊvəˈteɪk/
parade /pəˈreɪd/
park (v) /pɑːk/
Park'n'Ride /pɑːk ən raɪd/
parking fine /ˈpɑːkɪŋ faɪn/
road sign /rəʊd saɪn/
rule /ruːl/
salt /sɔːlt/
space travel /speɪs ˈtrævl/
stunt /stʌnt/
sunset /ˈsʌnˌset/
take up (v) /teɪk ʌp/
teach (v) /tiːtʃ/
theme park /θiːm pɑːk/
travel back (v) /ˈtrævl bæk/
Tree of Life /triː əv laɪf/
twilight /ˈtwaɪˌlaɪt/
under water /ˈʌndə ˈwɔːtə/
Which way? /wɪtʃ weɪ/

Unit 11

any /ˈeni/
anybody/one /ˈeniˌbɒdi/ /ˈeniˌwʌn/
anything /ˈeniˌθɪŋ/
anywhere /ˈeniˌweə/
balloon /bəˈluːn/
bark (v) /bɑːk/
become (v) /bɪˈkʌm/
earn (v) /ɜːn/
eve /iːv/
every /ˈevri/
everybody /ˈevriˌbɒdi/
everyone /ˈevriˌwʌn/
everything /ˈevriˌθɪŋ/
everywhere /ˈevriˌweə/
fancy dress /ˈfænsi dres/
get angry (v) /get ˈæŋgri/
get dressed up (v) /get drest ʌp/
get jokes (v) /get dʒəʊks/
get lost (v) /get lɒst/
get married (v) /get ˈmærɪd/
get old (v) /get əʊld/

Glossary

get tired (v) /get ˈtaɪəd/
get worried (v) /get ˈwʌrid/
ghost /ɡəʊst/
have a great time (v) /hæv ə ɡreɪt taɪm/
invitation /ˌɪnvɪˈteɪʃən/
laugh (v) /lɑːf/
nobody /ˈnəʊˌbɒdi/
no one /ˈnəʊˌwʌn/
nothing /ˈnʌθɪŋ/
nowhere /ˈnəʊˌweə/
present /ˈprezənt/
pyjamas /pəˈdʒɑːməz/
sheet /ʃiːt/
sleeping bag /ˈsliːpɪŋ bæɡ/
some /sʌm/
somebody /ˈsʌmˌbɒdi/
someone /ˈsʌmˌwʌn/
something /ˈsʌmˌθɪŋ/
somewhere /ˈsʌmˌweə/
streamer /ˈstriːmə/

CLIL – Earthquakes

edge /edʒ/
first aid kit /fɜːst eɪd kɪt/
hold on (v) /həʊld ɒn/
indoors /ɪnˈdɔːz/
outdoors /ˌaʊtˈdɔːz/
slow down (v) /sləʊ daʊn/
squeeze (v) /skwiːz/
stretch (v) /stretʃ/
wave /weɪv/

Unit 12

buy (v) /baɪ/
clothes /kləʊðz/
come back (v) /kʌm bæk/
forget (v) /fəˈɡet/
flight /flaɪt/
in ten minutes /ɪn ten ˈmɪnɪts/
keyboard /ˈkiːˌbɔːd/
laptop /ˈlæpˌtɒp/
meet (v) /miːt/
next /nekst/
remember (v) /rəˈmembə/
right now /raɪt naʊ/
screen /skriːn/
soon /suːn/
sunbathe (v) /ˈsʌnˌbeɪð/
work (v) /wɜːk/

Unit 12 - Curiosity Corner

addicted /əˈdɪktɪd/
bonfire /ˈbɒnfaɪə/
burn (v) /bɜːn/
doll /dɒl/
fill (v) /fɪl/
fireworks /ˈfaɪəwɜːks/
float (v) /fləʊt/
float back (v) /fləʊt bæk/
pour in (v) /pɔː(r) ɪn/
sink (v) /sɪŋk/
witch /wɪtʃ/
wizard /ˈwɪzəd/

Culture Spot 1

AD (*Anno Domini*) /ˌeɪ ˈdiː/ /ˌænəʊ ˈdɒmɪnaɪ ‖ ˈdɒmɪni/
army /ˈɑːmi/
BC (*Before Christ*) /ˌbiː ˈsiː/ /bɪˈfɔː kraɪst/
conquer (v) /ˈkɒŋkə/
East /iːst/
found (v) /faʊnd/
frighten (v) /ˈfraɪtn/
Hadrian's Wall /ˈheɪdrɪənz wɔːl/
North /nɔːθ/
public baths /ˈpʌblɪk bɑːðz/
South /saʊθ/
temple /ˈtempl/
tribe /traɪb/
West /west/
whole /həʊl/

Culture Spot 2

building /ˈbɪldɪŋ/
charter /ˈtʃɑːtə/
countryside /ˈkʌntriˌsaɪd/
environment /ɪnˈvaɪrənmənt/
healthy /ˈhelθi/
pollution /pəˈluːʃn/
settlement /ˈsetlmənt/

Culture Spot 3

behead (v) /bɪˈhed/
death /deθ/
defeat (v) /dɪˈfiːt/
factory /ˈfæktri/
fierce /fɪəs/
fire /ˈfaɪə/
following /ˈfɒləʊɪŋ/
huge /hjuːdʒ/
lasting /ˈlɑːstɪŋ/
railway /ˈreɪlweɪ/
rule (v) /ruːl/
sail (v) /seɪl/

Culture Spot 4

bat /bæt/
bounce (v) /baʊns/
compulsory /kəmˈpʌlsəri/
either... or /ˈaɪðə ‖ ˈiːðə/ ... /ɔː/
feather /ˈfeðə/
further /ˈfɜːðə/
grass /ɡrɑːs/
hit (v) /hɪt/
mainly /ˈmeɪnli/
outside /ˌaʊtˈsaɪd/
pitch /pɪtʃ/
shoot (v) /ʃuːt/
shuttlecock /ˈʃʌtlˌkɒk/
stick /stɪk/
tackle (v) /ˈtækl/
throw (v) /θrəʊ/

Team Up In English

Editorial Project: Sarah Howell
Eli Editorial Dept: Monica Gardenghi, Lisa Suett, Natalie Bayne, Maria Cristina Izzo, Sabina Cedraro
Art Director: Marco Mercatali
Eli Design Dept: Sergio Elisei, Fabrizio Redaelli
Picture Researcher: Giorgia D'Angelo
Production Manager: Francesco Capitano

Cover

Graphic Design: Paola Lorenzetti
Photo (left): British Museum, London - Marka
Photo (right): Shutterstock

© 2009 ELI s.r.l.
P.O. Box 6
62019 Recanati
Italy
Tel. +39 071 750701
Fax. +39 071 977851
info@elionline.com
www.elionline.com

The Publisher and the editorial staff would like to thank Janet Borsbey and Ruth Swan for their invaluable contribution to the glossary and the phonetic transcription.

Very special thanks from the Publisher and the entire editorial team go to Juana Cattunar for her precious support, detailed feedback and comments in every stage of the course materials' development.

No unauthorised photocopying

All rights reserved. No part of this publication may be reproduced, stored in a retrieval system, or transmitted, in any form or by any means, electronic, mechanical, photocopying, recording or otherwise, without the prior written permission of ELI.

This book is sold subject to the condition that it shall not, by way of trade or otherwise, be lent, resold, hired out, or otherwise circulated without the publisher's prior consent in any form of binding or cover than that in which it is published and without a similar condition being imposed on the subsequent purchaser.

All websites referred to in *Team Up in English* are in public domain and whilst every effort has been made to check that the websites were current at the time of going to press Eli s.r.l. disclaims responsibility for their content and/or possible changes.

While every effort has been made to trace all the copyright holders, if any have been inadvertently overlooked the publisher will be pleased to make the necessary arrangements at the first opportunity.

Printed by Tecnostampa 09.83.049.0

ISBN 978-88-536-0360-9

Acknowledgements

Illustrated by Laura Bresciani, Pietro Di Chiara, Andrea Goroni

Commissioned photography by Giuseppe Aquili, pp. 6, 8, 14, 16, 22, 32, 34, 40, 42, 48, 58, 60, 66, 68, 74, 76, 84, 86, 92, 94, 100, 102
With thanks to Harrow School, Harrow, Middx, UK

Student's Book photo acknowledgements
Darren Cox: p. 38; Harry Potter, J. K. Rowling © 2007, Scholastic, Illustrator: Mary GrandPrè: p. 61; Scott A. Dommin: p. 90; Marka: pp. 72, 114 (top), 115 (bottom); Olycom: pp. 23, 29, 39, 54 (top, bottom), 61 (bottom left), 80; Sherlock Holmes © Sterling Publishing: p. 61; Shutterstock: pp. 13, 23, 28, 33, 49, 50, 54 (middle), 55, 56, 57, 60, 61, 63, 64, 65, 69, 71, 72, 81, 83, 85, 91, 93, 101, 107, 108, 109, 111, 112, 113, 114 (bottom left), 116; The Weather Underground Inc.: p. 28

Student's Book CLIL acknowledgements
pp. 20-21, 72-73, 98-99 Damiana Covre, Melanie Segal, HandsOnLanguage, *Watch Out*, © ELI 2006
pp. 46-47, Damiana Covre, Melanie Segal, HandsOnLanguage, *Cook For Fun*, © ELI 2005 illustrated by Roberto Battestini